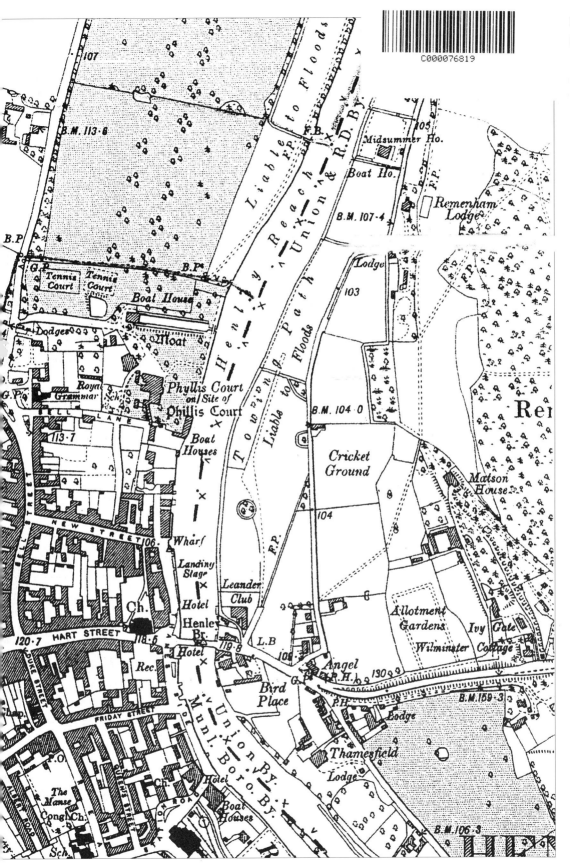

Ordnance Survey map of Henley published in 1927

V. H. HONOUR

HENLEY-ON-THAMES
A History

Henley on a busy day, c.1890.

HENLEY-ON-THAMES

A History

David C. Whitehead

Phillimore

2007

Published by
PHILLIMORE & CO. LTD
Chichester, West Sussex, England
www.phillimore.co.uk

ISBN 978-1-86077-452-2

Printed and bound in Great Britain

Contents

List of Illustrations

Frontispiece: Henley on a busy day, *c.*1905

Acknowledgements

The authors of the publications listed in the Bibliography have all contributed information used in the compilation of this account, and the books of G.H.J. Tomalin and G. Hollingsworth, both of which are now long out-of-print, provided the initial incentive to produce the present account of Henley's past. In preparing the book, I have also been helped by the knowledge and recollections of various residents of the Henley area, in particular Ann Cottingham, the late John Crocker, Roger Kendall, Tony Lane and Roy Pengilly.

I would like to thank the following individuals and organisations who have given me permission to include illustrations, either reproduced from their own photographs: Michael Hardy (128), Peter Parr (2, 3) and Peter Williams (66) or from postcards or other illustrations in their possession: W H Brakspears & Sons Ltd (48); George Bushell, whose collection of photographs that were assembled by his grandfather, a photographer also with the name George Bushell, is now held by the River & Rowing Museum, Henley (32, 53, 59, 71, 81, 106, 119, 124); Ken Clarke (7, 30, 33, 34, 54, 67, 80, 83, 121, 130); Paul Clayden (91); the Henley Archeological and Historical Group, who now own the collection of postcards and other documents collected by the late John Crocker (18, 19, 21, 24, 26, 35, 37, 38, 41, 44, 46, 47, 62, 74, 86, 87, 92, 110, 111, 132), as well as other illustrations (68, 85); Jennie Griffiths (99), Henley Royal Regatta (75, 76, 77, 78, 79), the Henley Standard (60, 84, 88, 94, 105); Henley Town Council (6, 29, 64, 65, 101, 104); David and Diana Painter (25, 42, 43, 70, 89, 96, 112, 117, 122, 123, 129); the River & Rowing Museum (13); Stuart Turner Ltd (49, 50, 51, 52); Way's Bookshop (4, 16, 22, 58, 72, 73, 82, 108, 113, 135, 137, 138); Barbara Williams (95, 114); and Richard Wilson (20, 23, 36, 62, 63, 102, 103, 107). In addition I thank Vic Mitchell for permission to copy the plan of Henley Station (69). Special thanks, too, for drawing several of the portraits and maps, to Judith Fletcher (9, 10, 11, 109, 118) and Angela Whitehead (1, 5, 8). Other illustrations are from photographs taken by the author (12, 14, 27, 28, 39, 40, 57, 90, 97, 115, 116, 120, 125, 126, 127, 131, 133) or from maps or other documents in his possession.

1

Introduction

All towns are, of course, unique in some way, but Henley-on-Thames has an outstanding combination of location, character and size that sets it apart. This book aims to provide all those who regard Henley as special with a better appreciation of how the fluctuations in its prosperity and status have given rise to the town as it exists in the early part of the 21st century. The surrounding villages and the countryside within a radius of about three miles from the town centre are also included in this account.

Its location by the River Thames and close to the Chiltern Hills, with Berkshire hills on the other side of the river, accounts for Henley's superb landscape setting. The course taken by the Thames through the hills from Wargrave, about three miles upstream of Henley, to Medmenham, about three miles downstream, is shaped like a horse-shoe and, as well as the valley of the Thames itself, there are several dry valleys that extend into the Chilterns from Henley or nearby. It is this combination of hills and valleys, together with a mixture of woodland and farmland, that accounts for the diversity of scenery within a few miles of the town. The town itself is in Oxfordshire but the land on the opposite bank of the river is in Berkshire and, less than a mile from the town in a downstream direction, is the boundary between Oxfordshire and Buckinghamshire. Henley's influence therefore extends into these other two counties.

The central part of the town has many attractive buildings that range in date from the 1400s onwards, with Georgian frontages being particularly prominent. As it is situated about eight miles from Reading and about 35 miles from London, Henley is to some extent a commuter town, but it also provides a range of types of employment. Nationally important companies in financial services and engineering, as well as many smaller companies, are based here. Henley still retains some of its earlier character as an Oxfordshire market town, and is a shopping centre for the surrounding villages. It has a monthly Farmers' Market in addition to a weekly general market. The ambience of the town is enhanced by some large areas of public open space, and by the presence of mature trees both in the town itself and on the road approaches to it, especially from the directions of Oxford, Maidenhead and Marlow. Henley still benefits from trees that were planted in large gardens and parklands by local landowners in the 1800s and early 1900s.

Henley is large enough to have a range of shops and services but is sufficiently compact for most residents to be within 15 minutes walk of the centre. Currently the population is about 11,000. There are two supermarkets, two doctors' surgeries, a local hospital, a library, a total of six primary schools, a comprehensive secondary school for pupils to age 16, and the Henley College for students of 16 upwards. There are societies and organisations in Henley that cater for a wide variety of interests and sporting activities. During the summer, tourism is important, particularly in July when the five-day period of the Henley Royal Regatta is followed by the Music & Arts Festival.

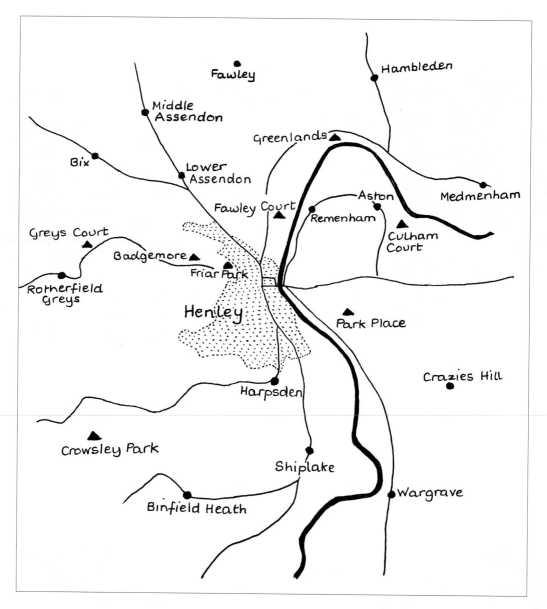

1   *Henley and the surrounding villages (●) and country houses (▲) within a radius of about three miles.*

The information in this book has been gleaned from a large number of different sources, the most important publications being listed in the Bibliography. Some of these publications provide much greater detail on particular aspects of Henley and its surroundings, and most of them are available either for loan or consultation in one of the local libraries. The Henley Library has a selection of books on the local area, while some of the older publications are available in the reference section of Reading Borough Library, in the library of Reading University or in the Centre for Oxfordshire Studies at Oxford.

2   *A view of Henley in 2000 from Henley church tower.*

3   *Another view of Henley in 2000: the church and bridge, and the* Angel.

2

Origins and Early Development of Henley

Before 1066

People have lived in the Henley area since pre-Roman times, as indicated, for example, by the Neolithic flints and pieces of pottery dating from about 2000 BC that have been found at Remenham. The remains of an earthwork, possibly dating from the Iron Age and forming part of Grim's Dyke, are still visible in Lambridge Wood, and it is thought that this ancient ditch and bank may have once marked a boundary between neighbouring tribes. Two swords, one from the Bronze Age and one from the Iron Age, have been recovered from the river bed at Henley and both are now on display in the River & Rowing Museum. Iron-Age settlements, in which each family lived in a one-roomed circular 'round house' based on a timber framework, were widespread across southern England and would almost certainly have existed in the Henley area.

Evidence of a Roman building at Henley, probably a farm, was found when archaeologists carried out an excavation in the area of Henley now occupied by the Waitrose supermarket. In addition, a number of Roman coins and three Roman urns have been unearthed in the town. Certainly there were substantial Roman villas at Mill End, near Hambleden, and at Harpsden. There is good evidence that a minor Roman road, possibly a branch of the road from London to Silchester, crossed the Thames by a ford or wooden bridge, near the present site of Phyllis Court, and continued through Lower Assendon, Bix and Nettlebed to Benson and Dorchester. Remains of the road, constructed of layers of flint, have been found at Bix. Crossing the Thames by a ford would have been easier in the years before weirs and locks were built, as the river would have been shallower, though wider, than it is at present.

The Anglo-Saxons took control of the Henley area from the native British (largely Celtic) inhabitants in the late 500s, after battles at Benson and Eynsham, and subsequently the two populations slowly merged. However, any Saxon settlement at Henley itself appears to have been small, though Saxon coins have been found at Bix. For most of the Saxon period, the Henley area was close to a fought-over boundary between the kingdoms of Mercia and Wessex, but it was agreed in the mid-800s that the river should form the boundary. Henley, if it existed as a hamlet, was then in Mercia. However, by that time, plundering by the Vikings had begun, the invaders arriving in this southern part of the country coming mainly from Denmark. The Saxons of Mercia eventually succumbed to rule by the Danes, but in Wessex the Saxon King Alfred negotiated a treaty in 878 by which the Danes controlled the land to the north and east of Watling Street while the Saxons kept the land to the south and west, including the Henley area. Then slowly, during the period 900-940, the Saxons regained most of England from the Vikings.

4   *Excavations at the Roman villa at Mill End in 1912-13.*

It was the Saxons who established the division of the country into shires or counties and some of the Saxon boundaries of counties and parishes have survived almost unchanged to the present time. The counties of Buckinghamshire and Oxfordshire were formed in the early 900s, and the section of the boundary between them, from Fawley northwards, followed the parish bounds that existed at the time; it still does so. Many of the lanes between Saxon villages and hamlets, especially in hilly areas such as the Chilterns, have also survived, some now as tarmacced roads and some as rough tracks. Another innovation during Saxon times, and one especially relevant to the Thames Valley area, was the introduction of water mills as a means of grinding grain, a process that was previously carried out by hand.

From William the Conqueror to 1500

After the Norman Conquest in 1066, much of the land in the country was taken over by William the Conqueror and granted to his henchmen, who became 'tenants-in-chief'. In return they had to provide military support to the King when this was needed. Despite the major changes in land ownership, some Saxon owners did keep their land, and others agreed to be become, in effect, tenants of a Norman lord. About 18 years after the Conquest, it was decided that a complete record was needed of who held the various estates that covered most of the country, together with the value of each estate. In some places the numbers of livestock were also recorded. The main aim of this survey was to maximise the amount of money due to the King through taxation, but the resultant Domesday Book has since provided a valuable historical record of that time. Much of the information needed already existed in the Saxon records of shires and hundreds, and so the King's surveyors were able to obtain the information about each estate quite quickly. And most landholders would have been keen to be included in the survey records, in

5   *Probable extent of the Manor of Bensington in late Saxon times (re-drawn from Pearman, 1896).*

order to provide evidence that they were the lawful owners. Domesday Book was produced in 1086: a modern edition was completed by Phillimore in 1986.

Surprisingly, Henley itself is not mentioned in the Domesday Book, implying that, if a settlement existed in 1086, it was not sufficiently important to be mentioned specifically. During late Saxon and early Norman times, the immediate Henley area was part of the manor of Bensington (now known as Benson) which was a large manor held directly by the King. However, the inclusion in the Domesday Book of the manors or villages of Badgemore, Bix, Fawley, Harpsden, Rotherfield Greys and Rotherfield Peppard suggests that the original manor of Bensington may already have been undergoing some subdivision. Other local manors or villages that were not in the original manor of Bensington but are mentioned in Domesday Book include Bolney, Lashbrook, Remenham and Wargrave.

In both Saxon and Norman times, life in the Henley area was almost entirely rural and based mainly on the manorial system. Each manor comprised an estate, of between several hundred and several thousand acres, whose peasant inhabitants were under the control of the lord of the manor. In some instances, this was the King himself. Most of the peasantry had the status of villeins, who cultivated their own strips of land in the open fields but also had to work on strips held by the lord of the manor. On average, each villein had about thirty acres to support his family, but most families lived in one-room dwellings made of wood and mud, often with their animals in the same building. The villeins also had access to common land, with rights to graze animals and collect firewood, but these rights were closely controlled. Some of the peasants, the serfs, had no land or personal freedom and were effectively owned as labourers by the lord of the manor.

During the Middle Ages, the system gradually changed, especially after the Black Death, which killed about one third of the people in Oxfordshire during the latter half of the 1300s. The peasants who survived had greater bargaining power and this was reinforced by the Peasants' Revolt of 1381. The villeins slowly gained the right to consolidate and enclose their land, and pay rent to the lord of the manor rather than work for him. In time, many of them became tenant farmers and eventually some became freeholders independent of the lord of the manor. However, while the lords of the manor relinquished some of their cultivated land, they increasingly took over the common woodland and grazing land for their own use. The woodland in particular

6   *Traps for catching eels (from Armstrong, 1884)*

provided a supplementary income through the sale of firewood and of timber for building construction. In manors that had access to a river, fish provided another source of food and, in some instances, income for the lord of the manor. Eels were numerous in medieval times and were often caught in traps that were placed at weirs. The manor at Wargrave is reported to have yielded 3,000 eels a year, and that at Remenham 1,000 a year. Mill ponds were also stocked with fish of various types.

In hilly and heavily wooded areas such as the Chilterns, the manorial system was less dominant than in flatter areas such as the Thames Valley, and life during Saxon and Norman times continued much as it had before the Romans arrived. There were small hamlets based mainly on a wood-pasture system of livestock farming, rather than large manors based on the cultivation of strips in open fields.

It has sometimes been assumed that 'Walter of Henley', who in the 1200s wrote an account of how to improve the productivity of agriculture, was based in Henley-on-Thames, but in fact he lived at another Henley, a village in Suffolk.

Henley's establishment as a town rather than a hamlet dates from the 1100s. It is reported that King Henry II (1154-89) 'bought land at Henley for making of buildings', and he would then have gained an income from rents, and from tolls that were charged for trading in the market place. Henley remained part of the manor of Bensington and was held by the Crown until 1199, when King John granted the manors of Benson and Henley (then mentioned separately) to a Robert de Harcourt. De Harcourt was the head of an important Norman family and he may well have encouraged the growth of the town as a river port and trading centre. By about 1200, a bridge had been built over the river, replacing the ferries and the ford that were used previously. The bridge itself was built mainly of timber, but with stone arches on each bank to support the timbers. One of these arches was still visible by a landing stage on the Remenham side in 1887 and, although subsequently hidden by building developments, was uncovered in 1984 during building work for the new Regatta headquarters. Arches from the Henley side of the bridge still exist in the cellars of the *Angel*.

By 1204, Henley certainly had a market place and a parish church and in that year King John gave the patronage of the church, St Mary's, to Robert de Harcourt, to whom he had already granted the manor. The patronage was acquired by the Bishop of Rochester in 1274 and remained with that bishopric for nearly 600 years till 1852 when it was transferred to the Bishop of Oxford. St Mary's Church was restored, with considerable rebuilding, in 1420 and much of the present building dates from that time, though some of the internal arches date from the late 1200s. To enable the bridge to be kept in good repair, the warden and bridgemen of the town were given permission to take the necessary timber from Windsor Forest, which then extended in the Henley direction as far as the Thames between Wargrave and Remenham. By the 1230s, a chapel dedicated to St Anne, a granary and several houses had been erected on the bridge itself, buildings that were similar to those on the old London Bridge, and the town had become a small riverside port.

In 1244, the manor of Henley, which had reverted to the Crown, was given by Henry III to his brother Richard Plantagenet, but the King retained, within his manor of Bensington, a strip of land leading from the main part of his manor to the riverbank at Henley. This strip included the route of the Henley-Oxford road, together with Bell Lane, and was probably retained to ensure there was good access from Benson, Wallingford and beyond to the wharves and bridge at Henley. It accounts for the wide verges along the Fair Mile which, as recently as the 1800s, were 'wasteland of the Manor of Bensington'. When the manor of Henley was given to Richard Plantagenet, there was a manor house in the area near Bell Lane, probably close to where the house Countess Gardens now stands, but it is thought that, after about 1313, the manor house was abandoned and eventually disappeared.

The layout of Henley, as it was established in the 1200s, is still reflected in the pattern of streets of the town centre. Two streets, now known as Friday Street and Hart Street, led to the river from what is now Bell Street and Duke Street, which formed part of the road between Reading and Marlow. In addition, Bell Lane, which is now a cul-de-sac, formed a third route to the river. New Street was added somewhat later, though before 1307. The burgage plots on both sides of Hart Street, and also on the north side of New Street and in parts of the Market Place, are further evidence that Henley was planned as a town in medieval times, though probably in more than one phase. Burgage plots reflected a form of tenure that applied to property in towns, whereby plots of land, with or without buildings, were allocated by the lord of the manor to merchants and tradesmen for rent rather than labour. The plots were often, though not always, long and rather narrow strips of land, behind or next to houses, that were used for activities such as stabling, workshops and gardening. In Henley, some of the burgage plots with their boundary walls still exist more or less intact but others have been built on, or amalgamated to form car parks.

The town grew substantially during the 1200s, and by the end of the century the church had been rebuilt with the large nave that still exists. The building and renovation of churches, and the construction of abbeys, were major features of life during the Norman period, and large amounts of land were donated to abbeys and monasteries. In the area around Henley there were abbeys at Medmenham and Reading, and a Benedictine monastery at Hurley.

Trade also increased during the 1200s, largely due to the expansion and increasing needs of London, and by 1269 Henry III had authorised the formation of Henley's guild of merchants. The main commodity leaving Henley was grain, much of which was brought to the town by pack-horse or cart and then loaded on to barges for transport to London. As an example of this trade, the manor of Cuxham near Watlington, owned by Merton College, Oxford, regularly sold its grain to merchants in Henley during the period 1280-1350. At this time, before the Black Death, trading in Henley is thought to have been dominated by merchants from London who acquired granaries and warehouses in the town, whereas later, in the 1400s, local merchants appear to have become increasingly important. Firewood, collected from the woods nearby, was another item that was sent to London. Edward I bought his firewood in Henley. A clerk was sent to buy 2,500 bundles in 1299, and another employee had the task of ensuring that they arrived safely at Westminster.

From the establishment of the town until about 1500, Henley was governed by a Corporation whose members included churchmen together with merchants living in the town, and by the early 1400s there was an official town clerk. The Corporation's most important responsibilities were to maintain the church and the bridge in good repair, using the income from renting out properties in the town. However, as trade increased, the Corporation gained more responsibility for other concerns of the town, such as control of the market and the appointment of constables. Among the regulations issued by the Corporation was one that prohibited butchers from 'throwing waste, hair, bones and blood into the street'. With the increase in the Corporation's responsibilities, it was inevitable that the lord of the manor, though still important, had less power than previously.

During the mid-1300s, the manor of Fillets (or Filletts or Filets), was formed at the edge of Henley and this had a manor house, Fillets Court, on the site of the present Phyllis Court, in contrast to the manor of Henley which by then had no manor house associated with it. The two manors were re-united in the 1600s. By 1480, Henley was sufficiently important for a Guildhall to be built and a market cross installed. The Guildhall was closer than the present Town Hall to the central crossroads, and is thought to have had two storeys with an open ground floor available for use by traders or shopkeepers. Alongside the Guildhall were the whipping posts, stocks and a pillory that were used for punishing those who broke the law. In 1485 stone blocks for the construction of Windsor Castle were brought overland to Henley from a quarry near Burford and then carried by barge to Windsor.

Several buildings in Henley have survived from the 1400s and 1500s, though all have been modified to some extent. They were constructed originally of a timber frame that had the spaces between the timbers filled with panels of wattle and daub. This mixture had sufficient flexibility to allow the timber frame to settle without undue cracking, and once the daub had hardened it was usually rendered with a lime plaster, and the whole building was then limewashed. One of the oldest buildings in Henley, and the one that has undergone the least modification, is the Chantry House, which still has some wattle

7   *The Chantry House, built in about 1500 (photographed c.1950).*

and daub panelling in its timber frame. It is grade 1 listed. It has a two-storey façade on the west side facing the churchyard of St Mary's Church, and a three-storey façade onto the car park of the *Red Lion Hotel*. The original roofing material is uncertain but the building may have been of sufficiently high status to have warranted tiles rather than thatch. While the present name of Chantry House implies that it accommodated chantry priests who sang masses for the souls of those who left money for this purpose, it is unlikely that chantry priests would have been provided with accommodation of such high quality. Also, recent architectural evidence suggests that the existing building dates from about 1500 (rather than 1400 as once thought) and was probably built as a merchant's house. However, according to the bridgemen's accounts, a schoolmaster associated with the church was holding lessons by 1420, and this may possibly have been in the Chantry House or its predecessor. Later the Chantry House was certainly used as a school.

The *White Hart Inn* is mentioned in records surviving from the 1400s but it was largely rebuilt before it became Henley's most important coaching inn in the 1700s. Another old building, the Bull in Bell Street, has some timber framing and probably dates partly from the 1400s, though it was extended and modified in the 1600s, and extended again and renovated in 2006.

Maintaining Law and Order

During the Middle Ages, each parish had to appoint a constable who had responsibility for maintaining basic law and order. Usually the parish constable held the position for one year, and then another 'able-bodied male' took over. In practice, the impact of the constable was limited as he normally had other employment and received little or no extra payment for his role as constable. Sometimes the person who was appointed paid someone else to do the job. When a crime was committed, local residents were expected to join in a 'hue and cry' to catch the offender. Then, if the offender were caught, he was likely to be punished either by being fined or by being held in the stocks or pillory, by a ducking on the ducking stool or by whipping. One of the constable's responsibilities was to keep the various items of equipment needed for these punishments in good repair.

Dealing with Poverty

In the Middle Ages most instances of poverty were considered to be self-inflicted and to result from idleness or wastefulness. Although widows with young children, orphans and old people were usually looked after by relatives or neighbours, other people without an income had to depend on charity. Adults who suffered a period of illness or unemployment, and old people who lacked support, often had to beg in the streets. However, in the 1400s and 1500s a few wealthy individuals did begin to fund almshouses to provide accommodation for those who were genuinely unable to work. In Henley, the first almshouses were founded through a bequest from John Longland, who had been born in 1473 in a house in Hart Street and who was Bishop of Lincoln from 1521 to 1541. The original almshouses, or possibly their successors, were pulled down when it was decided to widen the road between Market Place and the bridge in the late 1700s, and the present row of 12 houses to the west of the church was built in 1830 with funds from his bequest. Bishop Longland's mother, who continued to live in Henley, is buried in the Lady Chapel in St Mary's Church.

Transport and Travel

Throughout the Roman period and the Middle Ages, the Thames was the main transport link between London and the countryside that provided much of its grain, firewood and timber for building. Barges of various sizes were hauled up and down the river by gangs of bargemen – hard work which became progressively more difficult during Saxon times, owing to other developments on the river. Mills for grinding grain were being constructed on the riverbank, and these often had a weir across the river to ensure there was a sufficient head of water to turn the mill wheels. Fishermen, too, caused obstructions by installing barriers so that fish could be caught in nets or traps. The Norman authorities decreed that navigation should have priority over the needs of the millers and fishermen, but this ruling was difficult to enforce. In order to allow boats to pass, 'flash locks' were incorporated into the weirs with planks that could be removed temporarily. However, this operation was unpopular with the millers as it was followed by a period, often of several hours or more, without sufficient water for milling and so, to offset this disadvantage, the millers were allowed to charge a toll on each barge that passed through the lock. For the bargemen, going downstream through a flash lock was easy, though rather hazardous; but going upstream the barge usually had to be winched through the lock.

In 1274 King Edward I decreed that the Thames should be widened so that 'ships and great barges' could travel easily between London and Oxford. However, as well as the problems caused by flash locks, navigation upstream of Henley was made difficult by the limited depth of water; and the journey to Oxford was also slowed by a large loop in the river between Henley and Goring. The distance between Henley and Oxford is 50 miles by river and at one time there were 20 flash locks in this section compared with only five between Henley and London. Henley therefore became a terminal for the larger barges, with goods intended for Oxford, or coming from that direction, being carried overland to or from the wharves at Henley. There was a major packhorse route between Henley and Goring, and some goods were reloaded on to barges there for onward transport to Oxford. However, smaller barges were able to go beyond Henley, and both Wallingford and Benson had riverside wharves. The relative cheapness of river transport is illustrated by the costs, in 1304, of transporting a millstone from London to Witney. Having been purchased for 40s. 3d., it then cost 13½d. to load it on to a barge, only 2s. to transport it from London to Henley, and then 9d. to transfer it to a cart, 4d. for a toll at Wallingford and 18d. for two labourers and four horses to take it to Witney.

By the late 1400s, there was a regular barge service between Henley and London, as shown by the correspondence of Sir William Stonor of Stonor House. Sir William was a wool merchant, and he included wool as well as grain, timber and firewood in loads sent to London. He also ordered various items to be brought back from London to Henley, items that included dried and salted fish, wine, spices, glassware and, on at least one occasion, a silk gown for Lady Stonor. The barges usually took four or five days to travel between Henley and London, going downstream generally being quicker than going upstream.

Many of the roadways used during the Middle Ages were those constructed by the Romans though, once the Romans had left, these slowly deteriorated. Few if any roads with solid foundations were built until the early 1700s. During the Saxon and Norman periods, additional routes were established as rights of way between towns and villages, but little attention was given to road surfaces. People travelled mainly on horseback; and for the local transport of grain, firewood, etc., loads were carried mainly by packhorses or mules or, for short journeys, by carts. For these overland journeys, the rate of progress depended to a large extent on the firmness of the ground and hence on the season of the year and the weather, and whether the route followed a Roman road. The main reason for travel was to attend, as either a seller or buyer, the markets that were held every week in towns and the larger villages, or the fairs that were held less frequently. A number of packhorse routes converged at Henley due to its river crossing, and a few of them remain untarmacced and relatively unchanged today, though many others have been transformed into minor roads. Examples that show little change include part of Pack and Prime Lane, that runs from Henley to near Rotherfield Greys, and Dog Lane, that runs onwards to Rotherfield Peppard. Both of these were part of the major packhorse route between Henley and Goring.

Transport to and from Henley was, of course, encouraged by the building of the wooden bridge in about 1200. The Town Corporation, who were responsible for the bridge, appointed two bridgemen to keep it in good repair, using funds from the rents on various properties, including some buildings on the bridge itself. And, in 1230, indulgences were being granted by the Church to those who contributed to the repair of the bridge. Roads within the town of Henley were also the responsibility of the Corporation during the Middle Ages, but roads through the surrounding countryside relied on the appropriate lord of the manor and other landowners to organise any maintenance work that they considered necessary.

3

Henley during the Times of the Tudors and Stuarts

Henley as a Market Town

By the time Henry VIII came to the throne, in 1509, Henley was a well-established market town. Many of the inhabitants were involved in the barge trade, with grain, timber and firewood being the main commodities sent to London, while others were employed in the construction of boats and the malting of barley. Timber was essential, not only for buildings and boats but also for the numerous tools and items of furniture that were becoming more widely available. During Henry's reign, the town continued to grow. More houses were built, the wharves on the river bank were extended, and additional inns were opened. The prosperity of Henley is indicated by the fact that, in 1524, its residents paid in total the second highest amount of tax in the county (after Oxford city) and twice as much as Thame, the next most prosperous town. Henley was granted a Charter of Incorporation in 1526, giving its Corporation additional rights and privileges, and these were reinforced by another charter granted by Queen Elizabeth I in 1568.

Between 1568 and 1573, about one third of London's requirement for grain was transported via Henley. After 1568, Henley had the status of a borough and the Corporation consisted of a warden, two portreeves and 12 burgesses. As one example of its authority, the Corporation decreed in 1585 that the residents should not employ any workers who did not live in the town, if local craftsmen could carry out the work at a reasonable price. Under the charter granted by Queen Elizabeth, Henley also gained the right to set up its own gaol and for the Town Warden to be a Justice of the Peace. Parents were responsible for the misbehaviour of their children, and in the mid-1600s the parents of Henley children caught stealing wood or breaking hedges could be punished in the stocks, for two hours for the first offence and 12 hours for the second. If the offence were committed a third time, the parent could be whipped.

The area governed by the Henley Corporation was much smaller than the present boundary of the town, and extended from Friday Street in the south to Bell Lane in the north, with a loop between these two roads going around the upper part of the Market Place. The parishes of Rotherfield Greys and Rotherfield Peppard, whose settlements were, and still are, mainly on the hill ridges to the west of Henley, had narrow strips of land between Henley and Harpsden giving them access to the river. For Greys, the width of the strip was only the distance between Friday Street and Mill Lane, while Peppard had an even narrower strip between Mill Lane and the Harpsden boundary, and this strip of riverside included a water mill.

During the 1600s, the use of solid brick walls in new buildings became much more widespread. This change from timber framing with wattle and daub panels was encouraged

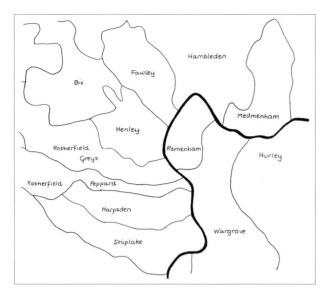

8   *Parish boundaries in the Henley area as they existed from the Middle Ages to the late 1800s.*

by a national shortage of good quality timber, a shortage that resulted partly from a large increase in the demand for shipbuilding and partly from the need to rebuild much of London after the Great Fire of 1666. Brick was also used as a replacement infill material for timber-framed buildings when the wattle and daub panels were damaged. Timber, of course, continued to be needed for roof rafters, and the increasing use of tiles rather than thatch for roofing had little effect on this need.

Many of the buildings in the centre of Henley, which are now shops and offices, were built originally as houses during the 1500s or 1600s and some have the steeply pitched tiled roofs   characteristic of this period. Bricks and tiles were made locally, and most of them came from the Nettlebed area, where the manufacture had been carried out since the 1300s. In fact, many thousands of tiles had been made for a renovation of Wallingford Castle as early as the mid-1300s, and the bricks to build the house at Stonor Park were purchased from Crocker End in 1417. By the 1600s, there were several family-operated brick kilns in the Nettlebed area, supplying bricks to both Henley and Wallingford, and the bricks were said to be of particularly high quality. Brickmaking at Nettlebed finally ceased in 1938 but a kiln about 50 feet in height was later restored as a reminder of the village's industrial past.

When Henry VIII decreed that the monasteries should be abolished, large amounts of land that previously belonged to the Church were granted to private landowners, a process that encouraged wealthy merchants to establish country house estates that were independent of the manors. However, parish churches were not affected by the abolition of the monasteries, and St Mary's Church was enhanced in about 1540 by the addition of the Lady Chapel and the tower, additions that were probably commissioned by Bishop Longland. Later, an effigy of Lady Elizabeth Periam, who founded a school for poor boys in Henley and who died in 1621, was installed in the church. It is still there. After the Reformation, the vicar as priest of the parish was made responsible for keeping registers of births, marriages and deaths, and in Henley these date from 1558.

Henley suffered a serious outbreak of the plague in 1581-2, with more than 100 deaths between September and February, and there was another substantial outbreak in 1625.

A problem that arose during the reign of Elizabeth I, and lasted until 1669, was a national shortage of coins (especially of half-pennies and farthings), due partly to the need for cash to pay the increasing numbers of men in the army and navy. As a consequence of this shortage, the government allowed tokens to be issued locally in order to facilitate trade and enable employers to pay their workers. Anyone who issued such tokens had to take them back in exchange for goods or services. At least 15 types of token, illustrated in the book by Peters (see Bibliography) from a collection now in the Ashmolean Museum at Oxford, were issued in Henley, three by the Corporation and the others by various traders and innkeepers. One of the traders was William Robinson, a fishmonger, and the collection includes a half-penny token of his, clearly embossed with his name, trade and the date of 1668. One of the innkeepers was the owner of the *Catherine Wheel*, an inn that was in existence in the 1540s and was named after the patron saint of wheelwrights. Eventually, when the government itself issued enough coins of sufficiently high quality metal, the production of local tokens was banned, and some of the people who held tokens found it was impossible to redeem them; some suffered serious hardship as a result.

Dealing with Poverty

During the reign of Elizabeth I, the government began to recognise that some, at least, of the people who were poor needed help, and as a result the Poor Law was passed in 1601. This law required each parish to appoint an Overseer of the Poor, and to levy a poor rate on the inhabitants so that those in need could be given assistance, either in their own homes or, if necessary, by being accommodated in a workhouse. In Henley, in order to meet the requirements of the Poor Law, the Corporation purchased premises in New Street 'for the use and benefit of the poor' in 1651. However, to qualify for help a person had to be near starvation, and individual inmates of the workhouse who were considered able to work were made to carry out jobs such as weaving, road maintenance or vegetable growing as a contribution towards their keep.

The Provision of Education

As Henley continued to grow it was considered to be of sufficient importance for King James I, in 1604, to grant a Royal Charter enabling a Grammar School to be established in the town. The school, which was housed in the upper storey of the building now known as the Chantry House, provided a small number of boys with an education in the classics. Until that time, the only children to receive a formal education were those in wealthy families who could afford private tuition, or the few admitted to a church school. However, King James provided little endowment funding for the Grammar School, and initially its main sources of income was a bequest from Augustine Knappe, whose will of 1602 had allocated funds for this purpose. Later there was an additional bequest from William Gravett. Although the Grammar School was described as 'free', payments had to be made for each pupil: on joining the school, 12d. had to paid to the master and 6d. to the usher, and thereafter there was a charge of 4d. per quarter. The boys had to learn Latin, and of the books listed as being in the school library half were written in Latin. In the school statute of 1612 was the rule that 'no scholar shall play within the School at any game at all'.

A few years after the establishment of the Grammar School, Lady Periam opened a charity school, on the lower floor of the Chantry House, where 20 poor boys were educated in 'writing, reading and the casting of accounts' to prepare them for being apprenticed. Four boys, aged about 10, were accepted each year for a five-year course, at the end of which they received money towards their apprenticeship. The bequests and endowments of both schools were mainly in the form of property whose rents provided an income that funded the running costs. However, although these two schools gave a basic education to some of the children in Henley during the 1600s and early 1700s, many children still had no schooling at all.

The Impact of the Civil War

The Civil War of 1642-4 had a major impact on Henley, and on several individuals who lived, or had lived previously, in or near the town. One of the first to become involved in the disputes leading to the war was William Lenthall, who had been born in the house in Hart Street now known as Speakers House in 1591. He was christened in St Mary's Church, though his family lived mainly in the village of Lachford near Thame. Lenthall became MP for Woodstock, and in January 1642 was Speaker of the 'Long Parliament'. In this role, when Charles I arrived at the House of Commons with the intention of arresting five members who were Puritans, Lenthall refused him admission to the House with the statement: 'I have neither eyes to see nor tongue to speak in this place but as the House is pleased to direct me, whose servant I am here.'

When the Civil War broke out in August 1642, the town was divided in its support for the opposing sides of King Charles I and Parliament, though many people were undecided and wished to avoid extreme positions on both sides. At the time, the most influential person in Henley was Sir Bulstrode Whitelock (1605-76), the lord of the manor who owned both Fawley Court and Phyllis Court, and his views were dominant. He supported the Parliamentarian cause, though initially he had been in favour of negotiation with the King

9   *William Lenthall, Speaker of the House of Commons in 1642, who was born in Henley.*

10   *Bulstrode Whitelock, Lord of the Manor of Henley at the time of the Civil War, and owner of Fawley Court and Phyllis Court.*

rather than military action. From an early stage in the war, King Charles had his headquarters at Oxford, and Henley was occupied for about three months by royalist troops led by the King's nephew, Prince Rupert. The *Bell Inn* at Northfield End was taken over by Prince Rupert and his officers, and they had a spy from the Parliamentarian side hanged on an elm tree in front of the building. The remains of an elm tree, claimed to be the one in question, were visible in the garden until 1995 when the dead stump was finally removed. The *Red Lion Inn* was also occupied by a Royalist brigade under the command of Prince Rupert.

For the next two years each side had several thousand soldiers in the Thames Valley area, attempting to occupy the towns of Reading and Wallingford, which generally supported the Royalist cause, and Henley and Windsor, which generally supported the Parliamentarians. Incidentally, Christmas Common, about six miles north-west of Henley, was named after a truce that was agreed there during Christmas 1643. The Parliamentarians did re-occupy Henley in January 1643 but not all the large houses in the area were under their control. As would be expected, Sir Bulstrode Whitelock's Fawley Court and Phyllis Court were held by the Parliamentarians, while Greenlands, owned by Sir John D'Oyley, continued to be held by the Royalists until 1644. However, during the fighting Fawley Court was attacked and occupied by Royalist soldiers who, against the orders of their officers, ransacked the house and vandalised Sir Bulstrode's library. Amongst the items destroyed were various title deeds and other documents relating to Henley and the surrounding area, that were held by Sir Bulstrode as lord of the manor, and as a result of their loss, there are now few records of Henley's earlier history. As Sir Bulstrode recorded:

> In 1643 the 4th of March, by the direction of Major General Skippon, Fillis Court house was made a strong and regular fort, and the Thames brought into the grafts round about it. Cannon, and a considerable garrison of about 300 foot and a troop of horse in it; and this was the rather done to watch the garrison of Greenlands which for a little fort was made very strong for the King, and between these garrisons stood Fawley Court, miserably torn and plundered by each of them.

Within the town itself the most serious military incident appears to have been the 'Battle of Duck Street' (now Duke Street), where, in 1643, a group of Royalists from Reading was confronted by a cannon, manned by Parliamentarians, at the crossroads in the town centre. In the fighting that followed there were casualties on both sides and eight individuals were killed. The Royalists eventually retreated. Apart from this episode, there was little fighting in the town itself but everyday life was severely disrupted. Both sides, when they were in occupation, demanded money from the inhabitants, requisitioned food and horses, billeted troops, attempted to gain recruits, and treated roughly any who were found to be assisting the opposition. The bridge also suffered considerable damage during the war, though this was due partly to the impact of a runaway barge.

11 *Prince Rupert, nephew of King Charles I, who commanded royalist troops in Henley during the Civil War.*

12   *This ancient oak tree by the bridleway at Henley Park must be more than 400 years old and would have been standing when King Charles I passed by after his escape from the siege of Oxford. (Photograph, 2006)*

Towards the end of the war, in the spring of 1646, King Charles escaped from Cromwell's increasingly complete siege of Oxford dressed as a groom to one of his supporters. On approaching Henley, the two men turned off the main route at Lower Assendon to go on a track through Henley Park to Hambleden Manor where they spent the night before travelling onwards. However, it soon became clear to King Charles that he had no option but to surrender to opposition troops.

Life after the Civil War

When the war was over, Sir Bulstrode Whitelock, despite supporting the Parliamentary cause and having suffered major damage to his property, refused to take part in the trial of Charles I that was organised by Cromwell. Nevertheless, after the restoration of Charles II in 1660, Sir Bulstrode was heavily fined for his activities during the war and, following an active life as a lawyer and politician, he retired to Wiltshire and died in 1676. One of his sons, William, occupied Phyllis Court and another son, James, took over and later sold the damaged Fawley Court. According to Thomas Langley, writing in 1797, 'Bulstrode Whitelock was a man of considerable learning, endowed with many valuable qualities, and of a mild and liberal disposition; zealous indeed of liberty but abhorrent of all those excesses which the abuse of it occasioned.' William Lenthall was re-appointed as Speaker in the Cromwellian Parliament but, like Whitelock, was not involved in the trial and execution of Charles I and, with some difficulty, procured a pardon from Charles II.

The war had severely depleted the wealth of many local landowners but Henley soon resumed its importance as a river port. Barge transport continued on a large scale, with grain, including malted barley, timber and firewood as the main commodities going downstream to London. The population of London had grown from about 10,000 at the time of the Norman Conquest to about 300,000 by the late 1600s, and this increase resulted in a huge demand for food, wood and other building materials. In Henley, the loading and unloading of barges, together with boat building, provided the main sources of employment, though there were also jobs associated with malting and brewing. A regular supply of beer was needed both by the town's inhabitants and by the bargemen who pulled the barges up and down the river, and there were several small breweries in the town. It was safer to drink beer than water at that time. Robert Plot was impressed by the construction of the malt kilns in Henley, 'so thriftily contrived that the kiln holes were placed at the back of their kitchen chimnies so that drying their malt with wood, the same fire serves for that and for all other uses of their kitchen besides'. In 1673, Richard Blome wrote:

> Henley has a considerable trade for malting, its inhabitants (which for the most part are bargemen or watermen) gain a good livelihood by transporting of malt, wood and other goods to London, and in return bring such commodities as they and the inhabitants of the adjacent towns have need of, at easy rates; and its market is very considerable for corn, especially barley which is brought there for their great malt trade, there being oft times in one day sold about 300 cartloads of barley.

A few years later, John Taylor of Henley Park agreed to deliver 1,000 loads of firewood to one of the wharves at Henley to be collected by a wood merchant from Westminster on payment of £540. And when the artist Jan Siberechts painted a view of the town, in 1698, he included a number of working barges. The view, as seen from the slopes above the Wargrave Road, clearly shows the tower of St Mary's Church, the old wooden bridge, two barges by a flash lock, and other barges moored by the wharves. There are also riders on horseback and a loaded hay cart on the roadway to Wargrave, and a stack of timber on the wharf near the end of Friday Street. This painting is now on display in the River & Rowing Museum. Jan Siberechts was an artist from Holland who came to England when he was in his late 40s and, during the next 20 years, gained numerous commissions to paint landscapes, many of them showing the country estates of wealthy landowners.

In 1664, more than 100 years after the death of Bishop Longland, more almshouses were built, a row of ten endowed by Humphrey Newberry. Another four were built in 1669 following an endowment by Mrs Ann Messenger. These 14 single-storey houses, which face the churchyard, were rebuilt in 1844-6, and were later enlarged by converting pairs into single dwellings, giving the present number of seven in the group.

The number of people travelling, and the amount of goods being transported, increased after the Civil War, and private carriages and wagons gradually became more widespread. These vehicles not only made deep ruts in the roadways but were liable to be brought to a standstill by thick mud. In 1555 the maintenance of roads had become the responsibility of parishes and, although statutes were introduced that required householders to give six days' unpaid labour per year for this purpose, the roads were still poor. Despite the difficulties, private travel was encouraged by the publication, in 1675, of a book entitled Britannia, compiled by James Ogilby, which included strip maps of

13   *A painting of Henley from the slopes above the Wargrave Road, by Jan Siberechts, 1698.*

14   *Almshouses, some funded by Humphrey Newberry in 1664 and others by Mrs Ann Messenger in 1669, both sets being rebuilt in about 1845. (Photograph 2005)*

various long-distance routes radiating from London. Although it was clear that road improvements were needed, little was achieved until the establishment of the turnpike trusts in the 1700s.

Religious Diversity

Religious differences were involved in the outbreak of the Civil War, and most Royalists supported the Anglican faith while many of the Parliamentarians supported the nonconformist Protestants, often known as the Puritans. One effect of the restoration of

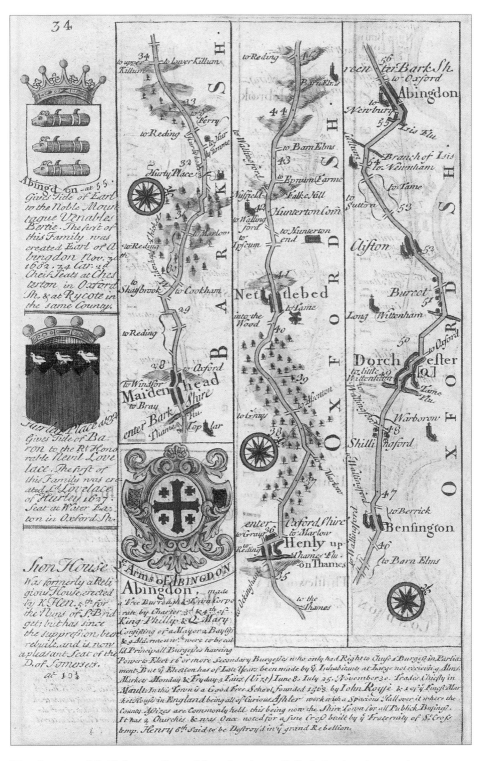

15   *A section of Ogilby's map of a road from London to Oxford, showing the route between Maidenhead and Abingdon via Henley, 1675. On the map, the route goes upwards on the left-hand strip and recommences at the bottom of the next strip.*

16   *The Quaker meeting house, used as a Youth Hostel in the 1950s and '60s.*

Charles II was that non-Anglicans (both nonconformist Protestants and Catholics), in Henley as elsewhere, were banned from holding any position in the town's Corporation, a stipulation that was not repealed until 1828. However, despite the ban on Protestants holding office, the years after the Civil War were marked by various nonconformists starting to preach in Henley. The origins of Christ Church in Reading Road can be traced back to the time of the Civil War, when local supporters of the Parliamentarians included Sir Bulstrode Whitelock of Fawley Court, and General Bartholomew Hall, who, when the war was over, bought Harpsden Court.

When a new Parliament was established under Charles II, it decreed that all clergymen should assent to specific doctrines and practices of the Church of England, and ministers who would not accept this regime were forced to leave their parish livings. The Revd William Brice of Henley was one of these. However, the nonconformists continued to meet in various unauthorised locations. In the Henley area, for example, they held services in Harpsden Woods, and the Revd John Gyles, who was another former minister of the Church of England, preached there illegally, but probably with the connivance of General Hall. On one occasion, the Revd Gyles narrowly escaped being arrested (and possibly imprisoned for life) by changing hats with a miller and then mingling with his large congregation. Itinerant preachers of the Quaker faith were also visiting various towns at this time, and one is reported to have preached at Henley on market days in 1658. However, by 1685 the nonconformists had become sufficiently established to be meeting in a barn by the Reading Road on land owned by General Hall and, as early as 1668, the Quakers were meeting in a building at Northfield End on the site of their present Victorian building. These meeting places became legally established in 1689 when the Toleration Act was passed and nonconformists were allowed to have their own buildings and preachers.

4

The Georgian Period, 1700-1837

A Time of Increasing Prosperity

During the 1700s, the country enjoyed a period of relative calm after the disruption caused by the Civil War and the subsequent restoration of the monarchy. However, there continued to be a huge disparity in wealth between the landowning gentry and most of the population. There was less discrimination against nonconformists and, in Henley, an Independent chapel was built in 1719. The town received a new charter in 1722, in the reign of George I, which introduced the titles of mayor and aldermen for the first time, and enlarged the town's Corporation to comprise a mayor, a recorder, ten aldermen (including the mayor), two bridgemen and six burgesses who were not aldermen, rather a large number of individuals from a total population thought to have been about 2,500. In 1722, the mayor was a George Harrison (whose namesake owned Friar Park about 250 years later). The Corporation was given the power to elect a High Steward of the town, and the first holder of this position was Thomas Parker, Earl of Macclesfield, who is reported to have negotiated the charter from the King. The 1722 charter gave the Corporation the power to hold a quarterly sessions for trying and punishing offenders, and it also stipulated that the bridgemen, as previously, should be the churchwardens of the parish church.

The trend for greater travel continued into the 1700s, especially after the introduction of turnpiked roads, and Henley became increasingly important as a stopping place for horse-drawn carriages and wagons. When the stage-coach service between Henley and London started in December 1717, the coach set out from the *White Hart Inn* in Henley every Monday and Friday at 6 a.m. 'with a good coach and six horses' and arrived at The *White Horse Inn* in Fleet Street late on the same day. However, for many years a major concern of the Corporation was the state of the bridge. No bridge is shown on Morden's map of Oxfordshire of 1695, presumably because even at that time it was virtually unusable and, although repaired from time to time, it had become so unsafe by 1754 that it was closed completely and the Corporation decided to purchase its own ferryboat.

That year also saw the publication of *Dycke's Dictionary*, which included the following comments about Henley:

> Henley in Oxfordshire, commonly called Henley-on-Thames, is the most noted town in the whole county; it is a large corporation town governed by a warden, burgesses and inferior officers; its market is weekly on Thursday, which is very great for timber and all sorts of grain, especially malt; the inhabitants are generally mealmen, maltsters and bargemen who carry corn and wood to London.

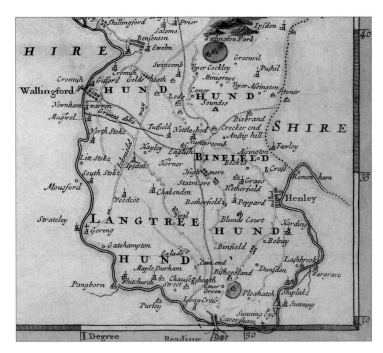

17   *South-east*
Oxfordshire from
a map by Morden,
probably published in
1722 and certainly
between 1695 and
1772, depending on
the edition.

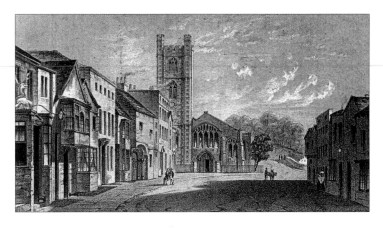

18   *Hart Street and*
St Mary's church,
Henley, 1790.

Malting appears to have been a profitable activity, as several maltsters were among the wealthiest residents of the town. The river frontage all the way from Friday Street to Bell Lane was occupied by wharves and wooden boat houses, while the buildings on the other side of the roadway were a mixture of warehouses, inns and premises for timber merchants and barge builders. A sign of increasing local affluence was the planting, in 1752, of an avenue of elms along the whole length of the Fair Mile by Sir Thomas Stapleton of Greys Court, who was lord of the manor of Bensington. In 1765 it was decided that no further use would be made of the pillory and whipping posts in the Market Place, and they were sold. The winter of 1775-6 was particularly severe, with deep snow drifts and hard frosts. Stage-coaches were almost immobilised for 10-12 days and Henley was cut off for this period. The Thames froze over, and it is reported that beer froze as it was drawn from the cask.

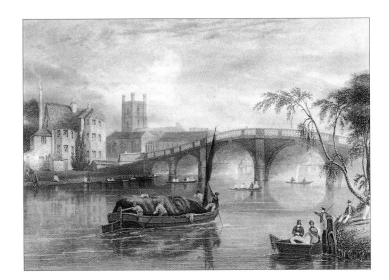

19 *Henley Bridge,*
soon after its
construction in 1786.

20 *Henley as seen*
from White Hill, from
an engraving c.1875.

A major flood in 1774 had finally demolished the old wooden bridge over the Thames and, as roads in the area were steadily being improved, there was a clear need for it to be replaced. The then lord of the manor, Sambrook Freeman, wished the new bridge to be built in line with New Street, but his views were overruled and it was sited just downstream of the earlier one. Although central, this position had the disadvantage of St Mary's Church preventing a straight approach from Hart Street. The new bridge was completed in 1786 and enhanced the role of the town as a stopping place for people travelling by coach from London to Oxford, Gloucester, Worcester and beyond.

In the 1780s the Corporation erected a tall stone obelisk at the central crossroads at the bottom of the Market Place, mainly to indicate the town's status. However, it was also inscribed with the distances to Reading, Oxford and London and so acted as a milestone. Close to the obelisk was a pump that provided water from a well for cleaning

21 *The obelisk in its original position in the Market Place, c.1870.*

22 *New Street, with the Kenton Theatre the fourth building on the left, c.1910.*

the Market Place and Hart Street, especially after market days. The obelisk remained in the Market Place for just over 100 years but was then moved to Northfield End.

The market was still important for trading in the 1700s but retail shops were beginning to compete with the stall-holders. The fairs that had been held regularly in the Market Place since the Middle Ages continued, and in the early 1800s four were held each year. They were an opportunity not only for buying and selling goods but also, at certain times, for hiring staff, especially farm workers and domestic servants. Individuals wishing to be hired displayed an emblem indicating the job they wished to have and, if successful, generally replaced the emblem by coloured streamers. The last Hiring Fair in Henley, which was held for many years in the month of September, took place in 1876.

In 1805 a lease on a building in New Street, that had been left to the Henley Corporation by Robert Kenton, was sold to Sampson Penley and John Jonas, both

23   *Henley's first Town Hall, from an engraving of 1875.*

of whom had some experience in acting and theatre production, and they decided to build a permanent theatre there. It was named the New Theatre, and opened on 7 November 1805 with a performance of the comedy *The School of Reform or How to Rule a Husband* by Thomas Morton. Although the theatre's first season was successful, its popularity was short-lived and, in 1813, the lease was sold. Perhaps the status of the clientele declined, as in 1812 a notice with the following message appeared at the front of the theatre:

> Whereas I, William Dicks of Newbury, bargeman did on Saturday night last, wantonly throw a Quart Mug, with Beer in it from the Gallery into the Pit of the Theatre, while the Play was performing, which might have materially injured persons sitting therein, for which offence the Manager had me taken into Custody, and commenced a prosecution against me, but on my making this Public Acknowledgement of my Offence and paying the expenses already incurred, he has kindly consented to stop all Proceedings; and I hope this will be a caution to all Persons not to behave in the like manner. William Dicks. Henley, 17 February 1812.

After the theatre had closed, the building was leased for a variety of purposes, including a school, a nonconformist chapel and a church hall for St Mary's Church. However, the building itself remained, and the Kenton Theatre is now one of the few purpose-built theatres in the country dating from the early 1800s.

Henley's role in the transport system made some residents increasingly prosperous and resulted in further changes in the centre. The old Guildhall, which by 1760 had slowly deteriorated and become derelict, was demolished, together with the Shambles, a row of cottages and small shops running along what is now the centre of Hart Street. It was not until 1795 that a replacement for the Guildhall was built, and this was known as the Town Hall. It was a colonnaded building in approximately the same position as

24   *The Georgian house in Bell Street, known as Countess Gardens, built c.1740 on the site of the original Manor of Henley.*

the present Town Hall, and a room in the basement was fitted out as the town gaol. It was designed and built by Alderman William Bradshaw and the first stone was laid by the mayor, who was then Robert Brakspear, the owner of the largest brewery in the town. At about the same time, the double row of shops and houses known as Middle Row, in what is now the lower part of the Market Place, was also demolished, giving a much more spacious appearance to the town centre. Middle Row extended as far as the obelisk at the cross roads and, before the building of the Town Hall, included the gaol and a pub.

By the 1830s, the Corporation's property portfolio consisted of a field let for £21, a fishery let for £21 and various tenements let for a total of £45, giving an total income of £81 per year. Of this, £4 was paid into a charity account while the remainder was used for items such as the expenses of the mayor, the salary of the Town Sergeant and repairs to the Town Hall.

During the relatively prosperous period from about 1740 to 1840, many new buildings were constructed in Henley and many that already existed were updated. A major objective of updating a building was to give it a new façade that reflected the style, now known as Georgian, that was fashionable at the time. Two particularly good examples of Georgian houses are those at 32 and 88 Bell Street, the latter known as Countess Gardens, while one of the best examples of a Georgian façade on an earlier building is the house known as Longlands at 39 Hart Street. Longlands and several other buildings in Hart Street and New Street have Georgian façades, of solid brick or painted stucco, combined with side and back walls of timber-framing infilled with lathe and plaster or with local brick. Local bricks were the main building material in Henley throughout the 1700s and well into the 1800s, though occasionally the brickwork was hidden under a stucco finish. And in the walls of some of the houses, and more especially in garden walls, flints were used in conjunction with brick.

The town began to attract professional people and merchants with sufficient income to build substantial brick houses on the outskirts of the town, for example on Gravel Hill and at Northfield End. In the late 1700s, Assembly Rooms were opened, and Henley had a social ambience of some style. The building that housed the Assembly Rooms is still in Bell Street, at nos 16-18, but its use for that purpose lasted for only 20 to 30 years, after which it became a furniture store. Private banks were opening in many provincial towns, and in Henley the Henley & Oxfordshire Bank was issuing its own banknotes in the early 1800s, though by 1821 it had been declared bankrupt.

At about this time, the built-up area started to expand along the Reading Road and on the south side of Friday Street into land that was then in the parish of Rotherfield Greys. A gas company was formed in Henley in 1834, with its works off Greys Road, and this enabled gas lighting to be installed. In 1838 a reading room was opened by the *Red Lion Hotel* where, for a subscription of one guinea per year, it was possible to read a selection of newspapers, magazines and reference books. And there were three Literary and Reading Societies, one supported by the local gentry and the other two mainly by tradesmen.

In the *Guide to Henley-on-Thames* published in 1826 there is an anecdote relating to the Assendon stream at a time when its underground section was under New Street:

> A little child playing in the street by the side of the stream fell in, and was carried with great rapidity underground the whole length of New Street to the river. Some men who saw the accident ran down to the river and reached it in time to catch the little child and rescued her from a watery grave, which appeared her inevitable fate. She sustained little injury, and lived to become the mother of a family.

Innkeeping and Brewing

The various inns in the town benefited from the travellers arriving by coach, and several of them were enlarged to meet the increased demand for accommodation. The *White Hart* was the inn that attracted most of the coaches providing a service for the public. By 1800, four coaches per week were travelling to London, and a few years later there were as many as 18 coaches stopping at the *White Hart* on some days of the week, most of them part of a daily service. Destinations included London, Oxford, Cheltenham, Gloucester, Holyhead, Shrewsbury, Stroud, Worcester and Birmingham, as well as more local towns. As well as providing accommodation for travellers, the *White Hart* had stabling for at least 70 horses. At one time there was a gallery along the west side of the building used for viewing 'entertainments' such as bull baiting and cock fighting. The gallery was later covered over, probably during the late 1800s. The *Catherine Wheel* was another inn patronised by coaching companies, whereas the *Red Lion*, rebuilt in the 1700s, attracted mainly wealthy people travelling by private coach. Among those who patronised the *Red Lion* was the Duke of Marlborough, who used to stay overnight when on his way to Blenheim Palace. The hotel's aristocratic clientele also included the Prince Regent, later George IV, who is reported to have once consumed 14 lamb chops at one sitting. In 1836 the *Red Lion* was praised by Edward Jesse in his book *An Angler's Rambles*:

> The mutton chops of my old friend Mrs Dixon are altogether unrivalled and she has the art of making all her guests happy and contented. I always enjoy myself greatly at her

25 *The yard of the*
White Hart Inn, *an*
important stopping
place for horse-drawn
coaches.
(Photograph, 1950s)

house, not only with reference to the beautiful scenery which I see around but from the real comfort and cleanliness of everything about me. Her sheets repose in lavender till they are wanted and her beds are neatness itself.

Another inn that attracted mainly wealthy people travelling by private coach was the *Bell* at Northfield End, which at that time included the house at the corner of Bell Lane, now known as Denmark House. In addition to the large coaching inns, there were a number of less expensive establishments, such as the *Bull* and the *Broad Gates*, that catered mainly for goods carriers and their wagons. The *Angel on the Bridge*, which probably dates from the early 1700s and was partly rebuilt when the new bridge was constructed in 1786, attracted the bargemen. In 1801 the landlord erected posts and rails on the riverbank so that their horses could be tethered nearby. As the *Angel* was built on land left to the town in the will of Bishop Longland, the freehold was owned by the trustees of the charity that he set up, and it is still owned by the trustees of the now merged 'Henley Municipal Charities'.

Henley was on the route taken by Karl Moritz, an enterprising young Prussian clergyman, who in 1792 was on a walking tour of England. After enjoying the view as he approached Henley down White Hill, he rested by the river but then found that even the smaller inns refused him accommodation for the night. He surmised that this was probably due to his rather bedraggled appearance but, whatever the reason, he had to walk on through the gathering darkness to an inn in Nettlebed where he was given 'a carpeted bedroom and a very good bed'.

Until the 1700s, the various inns in Henley generally brewed their own beer, obtaining the necessary malt, hops and yeast from local maltsters. Almost everyone drank beer and some households brewed their own. However, from the late 1700s, brewing became increasingly dominated by small firms who supplied beer to the inns, and Brakspears was one such firm. Brakspears Brewery originated in 1779, when Robert Brakspear's uncle, Richard Hayward, bought one of the small breweries that already existed in the town. Robert Brakspear became a partner in the business in 1781, took control two years later, and expanded it considerably. He adopted a scientific approach to the brewing process and this enabled him to produce a better quality beer than did his competitors. His success made him influential in Henley: he became an alderman and was elected as mayor on two occasions. When he died in 1812, he was succeeded by his son William, who also ran the business efficiently and profitably for many years. He too was an alderman and mayor, as well as being a magistrate, and was in turn succeeded by his sons.

The Social Hierarchy

A growing number of professional people could afford to buy their own property, but the nobility and country gentlemen, about two per cent of the population, still owned much more than half of the land and wealth in the country. Their estates covered most of the countryside. In the area around Henley, the nobility and country gentlemen and their families met at parties and dined at each other's houses, and those living at Park Place, Fawley Court, Phyllis Court and Crowsley Park all enjoyed a luxurious lifestyle. Mrs Lybbe-Powys, who lived at Hardwick Hall near Whitchurch and was sister-in-law of the rector of Fawley, made the comment about Henley in her diary of 1777: 'Never before was it so gay or so much money spent there.' Her diaries show that she was on visiting terms with the Conways of Park Place, the Freemans of Fawley Court, Lady Grandison of Phyllis Court, the Hodges of Bolney Court and the Halls of Harpsden Court. And trade from these wealthy families, and others such as the Stapletons of Greys Court and the Atkyns-Wrights of Crowsley Park, certainly improved the prosperity of Henley's shopkeepers and professional people. The opulence displayed by the local aristocracy reached its peak in the 1780s and '90s, when a young socialite, Lord Barrymore, was living at Wargrave. A masked ball that he organised to celebrate his coming of age had 470 guests, including the Prince of Wales and the Duchess of Bolton, but he was not universally popular and the *Guide to Henley-on-Thames* published in 1826 refers to him as a 'noble but inconsiderate owner'. Not all the money spent by the aristocracy was on short-term enjoyment, and at many of the country houses the owners spent large sums enhancing the estates for their successors. Scenically, the countryside was at its most attractive period in history, with numerous houses each surrounded by many acres of parkland, and large areas of woodland and common as well as farmland. We still benefit from the landowners' expenditure, as some of the landscaping and tree-planting carried out in the years around 1800, at Park Place and Fawley Court for example, makes a valuable contribution to the present-day landscape.

Next in the social hierarchy were the 'forty-shilling freeholders', whose property was sufficient to qualify them to vote in elections. They included clergymen, lawyers, merchants and manufacturers, as well as successful medical practitioners, engineers, builders and shopkeepers. A good example of a house in Henley built for an affluent member of this class is Northfield House at Northfield End. The rest of the working population were employed in jobs that included building, carpentry, innkeeping, shopkeeping, labouring and domestic service, and these groups were not eligible to vote. It was, however, possible for individuals to move up the hierarchy either through marriage or through being particularly successful in business.

26 *Northfield House, Northfield End, built c.1820.*

Despite the wealth of the aristocracy and the increasing prosperity of the middle class, many people still led a hand-to-mouth existence. In 1795 the Henley Corporation made appeals for the rich to subscribe to the relief of the poor and, although these appeals had a positive response, it was considered that food riots were a distinct possibility. In order to reduce the risk of violence in the streets, the Corporation obtained a promise from the authorities at Reading that they would provide support if this were necessary, but in fact the threat receded. As well as subscribing to the relief of the poor, the more affluent inhabitants of the town also donated funds for the defence of the country against a possible invasion by Napoleon. The Corporation passed a resolution stressing the need to maintain the safety of the realm and to bear true allegiance to the king, at that time George III.

This period of great disparity in wealth overlapped with the time when John Wesley (1703-91) was touring the country preaching at nonconformist churches. In 1719 the Henley nonconformists had an Independent Meeting House built near the site of the barn by Reading Road where they had worshipped since the time of Charles II, and it was at the Meeting House that Humphrey Gainsborough (see p. 104) was minister. On several occasions around 1760-70 John Wesley preached in Henley, and at least twice was critical of his congregation. In 1764 he wrote, 'The people here bear no resemblance to those at Witney. I found a wild staring population, many of them void of both commonsense and common decency.' At Witney, a market town about thirty miles to the north-west of Henley, he noted, 'This is such a people as I have not seen: so remarkably diligent in business, and at the same time of so quiet a spirit, and so calm and civil in behaviour.' Five years later he commented again on his Henley congregation, 'a great part of which was perfectly void of both sense and modesty'! But why did people of the type described attend his meetings? Perhaps, as has been suggested by Roger Kendall, they were itinerant bargemen who had little else to do.

Meeting the Needs of the Poor

Until about 1790 the workhouse was on or near the site of the present Kenton theatre but then a new workhouse, able to accommodate 150 people, was built on land that is now in the north-west corner of the Townlands Hospital site. Despite the increase in accommodation, the Poor Law arrangements still helped only the poorest members of society. During the Napoleonic War there was an additional call on funds from the

Poor Rate, as an Act was passed stating that the families of men serving in the militia should receive a weekly allowance. Recruits to the militia were chosen by ballot but those from wealthy families could provide substitutes. These additional requirements resulted in increased rates for householders and had a serious impact on those just above the poverty line. Some of those supported by the parish were thought to be better off than some who were working and paying rates, and in 1821 the Parish Vestry (consisting of all ratepayers in the parish), passed the following resolution:

> That in consequence of the great amount of Poor Rates of the Parish of Henley at this time, when, from the low price of all the necessaries of life the means of subsistence are within the reach of most men and the funds from whence the rates are paid are daily diminishing, it has become absolutely necessary to adopt some plan to remedy, if possible, this growing evil. And it appears to this Vestry that no plan can be effectual which has not for its basis the bettering of the condition of the poor and exciting in them as far as may be, a spirit of industry and a desire to exert themselves for the benefit of their families.

Some years later, it was reported that much of the income intended for the town charities was being used unconstitutionally to replace money that should have been raised through the rates.

The Poor Law was amended in 1834, with the result that groups of parishes, known as Poor Law Unions, were formed to take over the management of poor relief from the parish vestries and local justices. Each Poor Law Union had a Board of Guardians, with some members being elected and some nominated, and was expected to support one workhouse. All the workhouses built at that time were similar in design, having a central block for dining, recreation and laundry, with wings at each side for the separate dormitories for men, women and children. As with the previous regime, the Guardians had a basic problem: how to alleviate the suffering of the genuinely poor while keeping costs, and hence the poor rate, to a minimum. In general, the cost factor dominated, and conditions in the workhouse were sufficiently unpleasant to keep the number of applicants to a minimum. The food was poor, there was strict discipline and all those who were able to work had to work hard. In addition, families were separated and husbands, wives and children had to sleep in communal dormitories. In the Henley area, several parishes were grouped together to form the Henley Union, and the workhouse at Townlands was enlarged and rented from the Henley Corporation. Although there was then accommodation for about 250 people, the workhouse was soon full again. The master had a difficult role, being responsible for housing, feeding and clothing all the inmates who ranged from young children to the old and infirm. He had to keep accounts of the running expenses and of the income derived from work done by the inmates, and he had to arrange schooling for the boys and girls, with both groups having their own teacher.

The Henley workhouse building, with its 1790 datestone, still exists but has been rather neglected in recent years. In the grounds of Townlands Hospital there is also a small building that for many years housed an isolation unit, where people with infectious diseases were kept away from other inmates. This building was known as the pest house, and the poet Samuel Coleridge spent several weeks there in 1794 when, as a young

27   *The workhouse built at Townlands in 1790, and still in existence in 2007.*

soldier, he acted as a volunteer nurse to a comrade who had developed smallpox while their unit was on a march through the Henley area. The pest house is now in a semi-derelict state despite its being, like the main workhouse, a listed building.

During the early 1800s there was a movement of relatively poor people into Henley from the surrounding rural parishes, where the life of agricultural labourers was becoming more difficult owing to the enclosure of common land and the greater use of machinery. These local migrants tended to move into small cottages in the town that were being built and let on a low rent by speculative developers. Some of the cottages in West Street date from this time.

The Development of Medical Provision

After 1601, extremely basic medical attention became available free to those who met the local Poor Law criteria, but many others could not afford treatment. However, by the 1700s people who could afford to pay fees had a choice of three types of medical practitioner. Firstly, there were apothecaries, who practiced the 'trade' of medicine. Secondly, there were physicians, who were considered members of a 'learned profession'. And thirdly, there were surgeons, who were regarded as having a 'craft'. In addition, there were numerous quack practitioners, usually with less expensive fees but of dubious ability. To distinguish the more skilled apothecaries from the quacks, an Act was passed in 1815 which enabled the Society of Apothecaries to organise appropriate education for their trainees. Records in the Medical Register for 1779 show that, while Henley itself had just one surgeon/apothecary, there were several individuals of all three categories in the general area. In 1818 there was an outbreak of smallpox in the town, and the Parish Vestry recommended that all those who were poor should be vaccinated, the practitioners being paid for every person treated. A few years later, in 1823, a meeting of local residents agreed that a Medical Dispensary should be established, with both a surgeon and a physician, and the *Guide to Henley-on-Thames* published in 1826 lists three surgeons. However, the dispensary is thought to have come to an end after a few years, probably due to a lack of funds.

Although medical skills were improving by the mid-1800s, the cost of treatment, whether at home or in a cottage hospital, was still a deterrent for many people. However, practitioners were becoming increasingly professional, as indicated by the formation of the British Medical Association in 1835 and the legal requirement, after 1858, for all qualified doctors to be registered. The Royal Berkshire Hospital in Reading opened in May 1839, funded by contributions from local landowners and many other individuals in Reading and surrounding towns. Treatment there was free to those who were extremely poor but others had to pay.

Improvements in Education

Educational facilities, too, were improved to some extent during the 1700s. In 1778 an Act of Parliament united the Henley Grammar School with the charity school founded by Lady Periam under the management of one set of trustees, but they remained essentially separate institutions. The unification applied mainly to the endowments, of which those for the Periam School were in much better shape than those for the Grammar School. The schools were known as the United Charity Schools of Henley-on-Thames, and they continued to use the Chantry House until 1792, when they moved to buildings behind what is now known as Speaker's House, on the south side of Hart Street. By this time, the Lower School (Lady Periam's) was also taking some additional fee-paying pupils, probably the sons of tradesmen and craftsmen. A third school, the Green School, was founded and endowed in 1717 by John Stevens to provide education and clothing to four boys and four girls.

However, until the 1800s only a minority of children received any formal education at all, a situation that led the nonconformist churches to make schooling more accessible, especially to children whose parents were not members of the Church of England and were therefore not eligible for the church schools. The non-sectarian British and Foreign School Society was formed in 1808, and this organised the establishment of schools that became known as 'British Schools'. The Church of England then responded by forming the National Society for Promoting the Education of the Poor in the Principles of the Established Church in 1811. Managers of the schools supported by the National Society had to promise that their pupils would be 'instructed in accordance with the liturgy and catechism of the Church of England and would attend divine service on the Sabbath'. By 1820 there were both 'British' and 'National' schools in Henley, the former by the Independent Meeting House and the latter in the building that subsequently became the Kenton Theatre.

Improvements in Road Travel

In the early 1700s, Parliament made it possible for turnpike trusts to be set up, with the aim of improving the main road routes across the country and relieving the parishes of their responsibility to repair main roads. Each trust was responsible for maintaining a

28 *A milestone between Henley and Hurley, erected by the Henley-Maidenhead Turnpike trust in the late 1700s. (Photograph, 2006)*

section of a particular road in good condition and, for this purpose, was authorised to raise money from loans. The money could then be used to carry out improvements and could be repaid by imposing a toll on travellers using the road. Typically, the trustees included landowners with property along the road, possibly a merchant keen to facilitate travel along it, together with a surveyor and a lawyer. The toll charged to the traveller depended on his type of transport and, initially, wagons were charged by size. However the charge for wagons was later based on weight, and the turnpike trusts then had to install weighing machines at the roadside by the toll gates. The name 'turnpike' arose because the bar which was placed across the road to halt traffic was similar to a soldier's pike.

Three turnpike trusts operated in the Henley area. One was the Henley-Dorchester Turnpike Trust of 1736, which was responsible for a section of the Henley-Oxford road via Bix and Nettlebed. It provided an alternative to the London-Oxford route via Stokenchurch that had been turnpiked as early as 1718. The second was the Reading-Hatfield Turnpike Trust of 1768, whose road ran through the parishes of Shiplake, Harpsden and Henley (and then through Marlow, High Wycombe, Amersham and Watford) with a toll house (still there) about one mile south of Henley. The third was the Henley-Maidenhead Turnpike Trust, whose earliest records have been lost but which is thought to have been in operation by 1768, when the slope of White Hill was reduced in a project sponsored by General Conway of Park Place and supervised by Humphrey Gainsborough. From 1767, all turnpike trusts were required to erect milestones on their roads and some of these still remain near the roadside. There are at least three between Henley and Hurley, and two on the verge of the Henley-Oxford road between Bix and Nettlebed. These two lack their lettering, which was chiselled off during the Second World War in an attempt to confuse any enemy invaders. However, this precaution was not considered necessary by the authorities on the Berkshire side of Henley, and the milestones towards Hurley remain intact.

Once the turnpike system was established, the trusts often sub-contracted the collection of tolls by holding an auction for the right to a year's income from each toll. The sub-contractor, sometimes known as a 'toll farmer', having paid the trust in advance, would have to pay the wages of the men who actually collected the tolls, but was then entitled to keep any surplus himself. As an example of the sums involved, £800 was paid in 1830 for the right to collect the tolls at Bix.

At Henley, the bridge commissioners operated a similar system. When the new bridge was planned, loans amounting to £10,000 were raised to cover the cost. The bridge, which was designed by the architect William Hayward and was built of stone from the Headington quarries near Oxford, was completed in 1786. A toll bar was placed on the Berkshire side of the river, and the toll concession for the bridge was then auctioned each year in Henley

29 *A coach
with four horses
about to cross
Henley Bridge,
c.1790.*

Town Hall for amounts that varied from £600 to £1,000 per year. Horse-drawn vehicles
and farm animals crossing the bridge were charged, but there were exemptions for the
postal service, the army and local cattle going to pasture. The whole debt had been paid off
by 1873 and the toll was then removed. With the construction of the new bridge and the
introduction of tolls, the long-standing role of the bridgemen disappeared.

In 1798 the commissioners of Henley Bridge contributed £150 to the Henley-
Dorchester Turnpike Trust towards the cost of making a new road up Bix Hill, as it was
anticipated that a new road there would induce more traffic to use the bridge. The trust
then attempted to force people to use its new road by blocking the Old Bix Road from
Lower Assendon with an earth bank, but local residents objected, preferring to use the
steeper old road rather than pay a toll and the bank was soon demolished. Nevertheless,
the new road was further improved, and the trust constructed another length of road from
the toll house at Bix through the woods to Nettlebed to make their route more attractive
to travellers.

Although the introduction of the turnpike system had reduced the likelihood of delays
due to mud and potholes, travel by road still incurred the risk of attack from highwaymen.
The roads around Henley were particularly vulnerable to attack, as robbers could easily
take cover in the surrounding woods and commons. Highwaymen were also attracted
to the Henley area by the number of wealthy families. Mrs Lybbe-Powys mentioned in
her diaries of the 1770s that such robberies were frequent in the vicinity of Henley, and
that many of her acquaintances who travelled by horse carriage went suitably armed to
protect themselves (see the book by Climenson of 1899). In an attempt to curtail the
activities of highwaymen in the wooded Chilterns, a Steward of the Chiltern Hundreds
was appointed with the remit to catch as many as possible and 'hang them from the
nearest tree'. The stewardship became an 'office of profit' under the Act of Succession of
1701, and if an MP applied for it he had to resign his seat in the House of Commons.
Applying for the stewardship of the Chiltern Hundreds is still used as a method for MPs
to resign from the Commons. Robbery by highwaymen declined as roads became busier
and law enforcement improved, and had almost disappeared by 1800.

30   *The wooden bridge at Marsh Lock, taking the towpath to and from an island in the Thames in order to by-pass watermills on both banks. (Photograph, c.1920)*

Improvement in River Transport

The first Thames Commissioners were appointed in 1729 with the aim of facilitating the transport of goods on the river. Their remit was to impose some overall control on the operation of locks, and on the tolls that bargemen were charged for the use of locks and towpaths. However, the Commissioners had relatively little effect on the situation until 1770, when Parliament authorised them to purchase and replace by pound locks all the flash locks that had not already been replaced. Pound locks are the type that is still in use. The Commissioners were also encouraged to acquire the land necessary for a continuous towpath. Many landowners had refused permission for a towpath on their land and, as a result, the path often crossed from one bank of the river to the other, with ferries being used to carry the bargemen and horses across.

Even after 1770 improvements were slow, but the Commissioners were soon spurred into action by a serious proposal for the construction of a canal between Reading and Bray, which would have by-passed this section of the river and greatly reduced its importance for trade. By 1773, all the flash locks between Sonning and Marlow had been replaced and the towpaths had been improved, with the result that the canal proposal was abandoned. As well as making life easier for the bargemen, the new pound locks had the advantage for the millers that only a small amount of water was lost when a barge went through. The improvements in the towpath encouraged the use of horses rather than men for hauling the barges, a change that caused some rioting by unemployed bargemen. Horses increased the speed of travel, and in good conditions a barge could cover 35 miles in a day. However, the speed was influenced by the rate of flow of the river, and sometimes the barges had to stop completely. A resident of Reading recorded in his diary, in February 1814, that barges had been delayed for six weeks due to severe frost, and that bargemen had dragged a boat around the town begging.

Barge traffic on the Thames reached its peak in the period 1790 to 1840. The Oxford canal had been completed in 1790 and this enabled barges to carry coal, pottery and metal goods from the Midlands, via Oxford and the Thames, directly to London. Some coal was unloaded at Henley and other towns for those who could afford it. The barge trade also benefited from an increasing demand for paper, a demand which resulted in paper mills being built by the river. This in turn led to the necessary raw materials, rags and timber, as well as the final paper, being carried on barges. In addition, flour mills such as those by Marsh Lock and Hambleden Lock continued to provide work for the barges. The trade in malt continued, and a payment of duty had to be made to the local excise officer when this was transported. But if, as sometimes happened, the barge sank and the malt was lost, the maltster could reclaim the duty through the courts. On one occasion, a barge from Henley called *The Angell* sank at Marlow with about 34 tons of malt, and the maltsters received rebates that in total amounted to more than £80.

The remarkable wooden bridge that now takes the Thames Path to and from an island in the river by Marsh Lock, so that the path rejoins the Oxfordshire bank, was probably built when the pound lock was installed in the 1770s. Its total length including the section of path on the island is about 300 yards. It was constructed because a mill, probably on the site of the one in Peppard parish mentioned in Domesday Book, blocked the route of the towpath and there were two mills, known as Marsh Mills, on the Berkshire bank opposite. The bridge was robust enough to take the weight of horses pulling barges along the river and is sometimes still referred to as the horse bridge. G.D. Leslie, writing in the 1880s, stated that the bridge was threatened with demolition, but clearly this threat was not carried out.

The First Fire Brigades

There are two fire insurance plaques on the front wall of the *Bull* in Bell Street and others on houses in Friday Street and New Street. These plaques were issued, mainly in the 1700s, by fire insurance companies to indicate which properties had been insured with the company. In the case of the *Bull*, this was with the Royal Exchange Company. The plaques were embossed with the company motif and were often brightly coloured, though the two plaques on the *Bull* have now been painted black. They were fixed in a prominent position on the front of the building so that they were easy for the firemen to identify. The insurance companies recruited their own local part-time fire brigades and, when a fire broke out, the firemen were expected to hurry to the scene. If the building appeared not to be insured by their company, they would leave it to burn, or they might cheer or jeer at the brigade actually fighting the fire. In time, the insurance companies decided that it would be better to pool their resources and merge their local brigades, and so the number of individual units declined.

The Beginnings of Team Sports

Cricket was probably the first organised team game to be played in Henley. A match played in August 1766 between Henley and a team composed of a Mr Matthew Slaughter and his ten sons was reported in the *Reading Mercury*. A county match, Oxfordshire vs. Berkshire, was played at Henley in 1779.

5

Henley's Rapid Expansion, 1837-1914

From Boom to Bust and Boom again

The prosperity of the stage-coach period came to an abrupt end with the opening of the railway from London to Reading and Bristol in 1840-1 and, although the railway did not at that time come to Henley, it soon resulted in a surge of unemployment among Henley's population, which according to the census of 1841 numbered 3,622. Workers in the coaching inns and in the shops were the worst affected. About ten per cent of the houses in the town were unoccupied, poverty was widespread and some assistance for the unemployed was provided by a soup kitchen set up at the Town Hall. The *Reading Mercury and Oxford Gazette* of 1 July 1848 reported that the inhabitants of Henley sent a petition to the House of Commons, stating:

> That in consequence of the diversion of road traffic which once passed through the town, but is now conveyed by the Great Western Railway, the trade of the town has very materially decreased, that the burden of the poor has at the same time very much increased. That your petitioners have felt the Income Tax to press heavily upon them and … they pray that your honourable house would take into consideration the whole question of taxation with a view to every practical reduction.

The *Bell Inn* closed permanently, and the *Red Lion* was closed for seven years during the 1850s.

Another consequence of the developing railway network was that fresh fish from the sea could be distributed around the country, and the river fishing industry therefore began to decline. By 1861, trade in Henley had declined to such an extent that the landlord of the *White Hart* was described as a baker as well as an innkeeper. However, the town's agricultural market continued to be busy, and some of the less expensive inns were supported by the corn merchants and carriers who came to the market.

Despite Henley's loss of trade, some aspects of life did improve during the mid-to late 1800s. There was a supply of gas for lighting, as mentioned in the previous chapter, and by 1850 there was a post office in the town, at a shop at 11 Market Place that also sold stationery and medicines. Another improvement was the construction of the town's waterworks in 1882 and hence a supply of piped clean water. The water was obtained from a 240 ft deep well in the chalk and was pumped first to a reservoir on Badgemore Hill. Previously, all householders had obtained water from their own wells, from underground storage tanks in which rainwater from roofs was collected or from the main town well near the obelisk. A sewerage system was installed in the town in 1886.

109

POST-OFFICE, HENLEY.

The box for the receipt of Letters closes at half-past seven o'clock in the Evening, from which Time until eight, a fee of one Penny must be paid with each Letter, after which no Letter can be forwarded.

Letters for Town or Local Delivery, are liable to the same rate of charge as those sent by the General Post.

Turville, Hambleden, Checkendon and Peppard.

Postmen for the above Places, leave the Office every Morning from March 1st to October 31st, at Seven o'Clock, and return in the Afternoon at Four. The other four Months they leave at Half-past Seven in the Morning, and return at Half-past Three in the Afternoon.

Boxes for the reception and payment of Letters, are open at Mr. Green's Turville; Mr. Bigg's, Hambleden; Mr. Hope's, Checkendon; & Mr. Reeves's Peppard.

Nettlebed.

Letters for Nettlebed and its Vicinity, are forwarded by Postman every Morning, at a Quarter-past Six who returns the same Evening at Half-past Six *precisely*.

Wargrave.

Letters for Wargrave are forwarded by Postman every Morning at Seven o'Clock, from November 1st. to March 1st. and Half-past Six the other eight months. Returns every Evening at Half-past Six *precisely*.

A Box for the reception and **payment of Letters** is open at Mr. Toomer's.

Photograph   G. Bushell & Son, Henley
HENLEY'S FIRST POSTMAN.
(Date shortly after 1840 as adhesive stamps are on letters.)

31 *Local Post Office services as provided in 1838, and advertised in the* Guide to Henley upon Thames *of that date.*

32 *Henley's first postman, photographed during the 1850s.*

After the annual regatta had received royal patronage from Queen Victoria and Prince Albert in 1851, Henley slowly became more popular again, though mainly as a destination for day-trips and for holidays. Eventually the *Red Lion* re-opened, became profitable again and was sold by Brakspears Brewery in 1888-9 to a Mr Shepherd, who converted what was a stable block facing the river into a boathouse. Boats for hire were available from the ground floor, while a boat-building business, in which Mr Shepherd was a partner, was active on the first floor. During the years around 1900, the heyday of the Regatta, the *Red Lion* was described as a fashionable hotel and its lawn, across the road by the riverbank, was sufficiently spacious to accommodate several tables at which afternoon tea was served. The *Catherine Wheel*, too, soon adapted to the new circumstances: it provided 'an omnibus and carriages to meet all trains', and its guests could use an excellent billiard room. Another hotel, the *White Hart*, also changed successfully from a coaching inn to a hotel for travellers by train and later by car. The *Bull* continued to attract custom from local goods carriers, and in 1863 was advertised as having stables for about sixty horses. As horse traffic declined, it gradually became a local pub, as did other smaller inns.

The renewed popularity of the town during the period 1870 to 1900 resulted in the construction of three new hotels, the *Royal* (now Royal Mansions), the *Little White Hart* (now a shop and apartments) and the *Imperial*, all built in the half-timbered style that was fashionable at the time. The *Imperial Hotel* was built in 1897 opposite the station, a location chosen in order to attract visitors arriving by train. Shops were built on each side, and the roof of the hotel was decorated by a finial in the shape of a dragon.

33 *The* Red Lion Hotel *with its lawn on which afternoon tea was served, c.1910.*

34 *Above: The* Catharine Wheel Hotel, *c.1900 – note the spelling 'Catharine' which was in use from the mid-1600s to the early 1900s.*

35 *Left: The* Imperial Hotel, *built in 1897. (Photographed c.1920)*

36 *St Mark's Road in 1906, showing houses recently built by Richard Wilson above the junction with Vicarage Road.*

37 *Kings Road, with houses built c.1900.*

The town also became more desirable as a place to live, especially after the Henley-Twyford branch line had opened in 1857 (see p.65). To meet the demand, a Henley Building Company was formed in 1864 and more houses were built, for example in Gravel Hill. After the arrival of the railway, many of the new houses were constructed of bricks brought in by train that were harder and more uniform than those made locally, and Welsh slate was used for roofing. Increasingly, the additional housing was built to the south of the town, with larger houses in the St Andrew's Road/ St Mark's Road/ Vicarage Road area, and with smaller terraced houses in and near to Reading Road, Harpsden Road and King's Road. The larger houses had substantial gardens, and a number of trees planted in them still benefit the appearance of the town.

Significant Henley buildings that date entirely from the Victorian period include the four pairs of large semi-detached villas, once known as the Oxford Villas, at the beginning of the Fair Mile. They also include River Terrace, the row of seven tall stuccoed houses

38   *Left: River
Terrace, built c.1866.
(Photograph, c.1920)*

39   *Below left:
A house in Queen
Street, decorated in
Arts and Crafts style,
built c.1900.*

on Thameside south, built in 1866. Both groups were intended for affluent middle-class families with domestic staff. Most of the first group have since been extended and are now mainly offices and apartments, and most of the second group have been sub-divided into apartments. A row of boathouses with first-floor balconies was built in Wharfe Lane by Hobbs and Sons, to replace the previous wooden buildings and to provide viewpoints for the Regatta. They have since been converted entirely to residential accommodation.

New buildings dating from the years around 1900 include the large detached houses in Norman Avenue and the three pairs of semi-detached houses, decorated in the Arts and Crafts style, in Queen Street. The houses in Norman Avenue were built by Charles Clements, and they incorporate some stone blocks thought to have been discarded from the building of the house at Friar Park due to last-minute changes in design. The façades of the houses in Norman Avenue also include some unusual decorative features such as turrets and carved woodwork. Fortunately for the present character of Henley, further expansion of the town to the north and west, in the directions of Badgemore, Assendon and Hambleden, was curtailed by the existence of the parklands at Friar Park, Henley Park and Fawley Court.

During the Victorian period, other Henley buildings were altered by the addition of timber-framed facades. This type of alteration can be seen in Hart Street and Market Place, one example being the Speakers House in Hart Street which was originally built in the 1500s. Here, as in most of the timber-framed buildings, the timbers have been treated with a dark stain or black paint, but this practice began only in the 1800s.

There was a major increase in the town's population during the 1800s and early 1900s. In 1801, the national census recorded a population of 2,948, but by 1911 this had increased to 6,456, a figure that reflects partly the natural increase, partly the movement of people from villages to the town, and partly the extension of the town boundary in 1892 (see p. 53). With the growth in Henley's population, it was decided in 1870 to enlarge the Town Hall by enclosing part of the ground floor that had previously been used as a corn market. Despite this, a few years later the Henley Corporation thought that a larger building was necessary, and the old Town Hall was dismantled and rebuilt, with some modifications, as a private house by Charles Clements. He was mayor of Henley at the time and chose to erect his new house at Crazies Hill. The present Town Hall was then built to mark Queen Victoria's Diamond Jubilee and was completed in March 1901. It incorporates a foundation stone laid by the Hon. W.F.D. Smith MP, the son of W.H. Smith and a major contributor to the building fund.

40   *Houses in Norman Avenue, built in c.1900. (Photograph, 2006)*

The increasing population to the south of the town led to Duke Street being widened in 1872, by demolishing and then rebuilding the houses on its west side. This project was instigated by J.S. Burn, who wrote a history of Henley that was published in 1861. Further improvements to the town centre were carried out in the 1890s when the Corporation widened at least two narrow road junctions by replacing some of the buildings with others set further back from the roadway. Thus, a new curved façade was installed at the corner of Hart Street and Bell Street, and the building at 1-7 Greys Road, though completely different in style, had a similar effect. In 1895 a new purpose-built post office was opened in Reading Road, on the corner with Friday Street, replacing the previous one in the Market Place. This building is now occupied by the Lloyds TSB Bank.

The drinking fountain which is now outside St Mary's Church by the almshouses was originally erected in the Market Place in 1885 in memory of the Revd Greville Phillimore. He was the rector of Henley from 1867 to 1883 and made various donations to the town. The fountain, which is constructed partly of a reddish rock, porphyry, displaced the obelisk from the Market Place and resulted in it being moved to Northfield End. While the fountain was in the Market Place, its steps were used as a stall by people selling lavender, a plant grown commercially in the grounds of Park Place. However, by 1903 the fountain was considered to be obstructing the flow of traffic in the town centre, and it was transferred to its present position by the church.

In 1894-5 Henley was hit by the worst flooding for more than a hundred years, and some of the buildings by the river, including the *Little White Hart*, were flooded to a depth of two feet or more, as indicated by the marker stone inserted into the wall of 11 Thameside.

41   *Duke Street before its widening in 1872.*

Commercial Activities

With the growth in Henley's population, there was also a growth in commercial activity, and Emily Climenson's book of 1896 lists malting, brewing, wood sawing, an iron foundry, a paper bag manufactory and the making of boats. The map that she produced shows the layout of the town at that time with the location of various important buildings. Both the foundry and the paper bag factory were in Friday Street, the former in what is now the house 'Old Foundry', and the factory in the brick building on the north-west side, almost opposite the end of Queen Street.

During the 1800s, the brewery firms began to take over various inns and beer-houses, so that the inns were then tied to a particular brewer and the occupant became a tenant and licensee of the brewery. Henley has always been well supplied with pubs, inns and hotels, and as many as 137 buildings, or sites of previous buildings, have been identified by Ann Cottingham as being at some time a pub, an inn, a hotel or just a beerhouse. In 1852, the ratio of pubs to population in Henley was 1:80, an exceptional figure even then, as the national ratio was about 1:200. The brewery firms themselves also began to consolidate, and in 1896 Brakspears, having become a public company, took over and then closed down its main rival Greys Brewery, which was on the south side of Friday Street. Brakspears then owned 150 pubs. From 1852 to 1882, William Brakspear lived at Paradise House, a large house with a splendid view across the town to Park Place, but of which the only remaining visible evidence is the high brick and flint garden wall with two gateways on to Gravel Hill.

Later, in about 1900, Brakspears built the large malthouse on New Street opposite the brewery and this enabled them to sell or lease their other malthouses in the town. Malting was continued at New Street until 1972, when a maltster with long experience retired, after which malt for the brewery was brought into the town and the malthouse

42 *The Post Office, in a building now occupied by Lloyds TSB Bank, at the corner of Reading Road and Friday Street; Southfield House (opposite) was demolished in 1921. (Photograph, c.1910)*

43 *The fountain that displaced the obelisk from the Market Place in 1885.*

44 *Flooding at the* Little Angel, *probably in 1894-5.*

was converted into offices. After the death of William Brakspear in 1882, two of his sons, Archibald and George, took over, and they had a new set of buildings erected. George Brakspear also became involved in local government, and was elected as the first chairman of the Henley Rural District Council formed in 1894. The brewery buildings in New Street were completed in 1897 and are typical of brewery architecture of the late Victorian period, with walls of red engineering brick and windows in arched recesses. The external appearance of the buildings, including a rectangular stone block in the wall facing New Street inscribed 'WHB and Sons 1897', was retained in the redevelopment that was carried out from 2004 onwards. One of the buildings was converted into a hotel and bistro, others have been converted into offices, while others have been replaced by apartments.

Another important Henley business started in 1897, when Mr Sidney Stuart Turner was appointed to the staff at Shiplake Court and put in charge of a domestic electricity generating plant. Here, as in some other houses of wealthy individuals, a boiler and high speed steam engine were being installed to drive a dynamo that generated sufficient electricity for lighting. In his spare time, Mr Stuart Turner designed and sold model steam engines, and after a few years this sideline became so successful that he was able to resign from his original position. He set up Stuart Turner Ltd with a few other engine enthusiasts in 1908, and in 1911 the firm started to make and sell motor cycles. They extended their premises in the Market Place into the old *Broad Gates Inn* in 1917, when they had 400 employees, mainly girls, making military equipment for the First World War. The *Broad Gates* was one of the oldest inns in Henley and, until it closed, was popular with farmers on market days. Despite his success, Mr Stuart Turner left the firm in 1920 and emigrated to South Africa, but the business continued and, in the Second World War, the staff worked in shifts, day

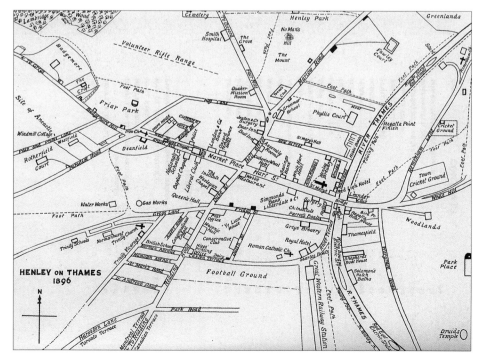

45   *A map of Henley published by Climenson in 1896.*

46   *Workers in the iron foundry, Friday Street, early 1900s.*

47   *Inside the paper bag factory and printing works, Friday Street, early 1900s.*

48   Brakspears Brewery, with a delivery cart in the early 1900s.

49   Mr Sidney Stuart Turner on his 50th birthday in 1918 (courtesy of Stuart Turner Ltd).

50   The Stuart Turner Ltd 'Stellar' motorbike produced in 1912 (courtesy of Stuart Turner Ltd).

51   The premises of Stuart Turner Ltd, 'Shiplake Works' in Henley, with a cart loaded with goods for onward transport by the Great Western Railway, and the Broad Gates inn in the background, c.1914 (courtesy of Stuart Turner Ltd).

52 *Staff employed at Stuart Turner Ltd, photographed in 1916 (courtesy of Stuart Turner Ltd).*

and night, producing marine engines and generators. The firm now manufactures a wide range of pumping equipment, much of which is exported around the world.

Until Victorian times, the water mill on the south side of Marsh Lock was used for grinding grain but subsequently it was used as a paper mill and, later, a brass foundry.

Changes in Local Government

Until 1883 Henley continued to operate more or less according to the 1722 charter. This was despite the Municipal Reform Act of 1832 and the Corporation Reform Act of 1835, which extended the right to vote to all those who owned or leased buildings of a certain value, whereas previously the right to vote had been restricted to a few extremely wealthy landowners. In 1867 the franchise was extended again, this time to all male householders in towns, though not to sons or lodgers living in the same house, but again this change had little impact in Henley, where the major landowners in the locality dominated society. Nevertheless, over the next few decades, local government did slowly become more democratic. The existing Corporation was dissolved in 1883, and a new charter confirmed the town's status as a municipal borough and stipulated that the Corporation should consist of a mayor, four aldermen and 12 councillors, the mayor being one of the aldermen or councillors.

County councils were created in 1888, together with county boroughs such as Reading. Then, in 1894, the Local Government Act created new parish councils, and also larger local authorities known as urban and rural district councils. The district councils included Henley Urban DC and Henley Rural DC, the latter with a total of 18 parishes. By this time, the members of Henley Town Council included a number of tradesmen, but Henley Rural District continued to be dominated by the major landowners who had been members of the Rural Sanitary Authority set up in 1872. In the Rural District Council election of 1894, only three of the 18 parishes were contested. The county councils, and the urban and rural district councils, slowly gained more influence through

53   *A meeting of the Henley Borough Council at the Town Hall in 1895.*

54   *The Fair Mile with its verges being grazed by sheep, 1903.*

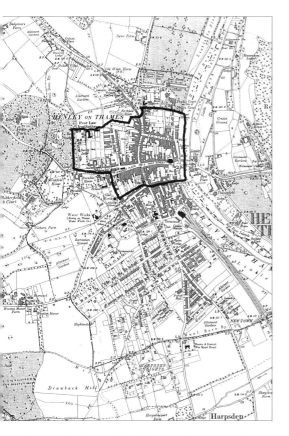

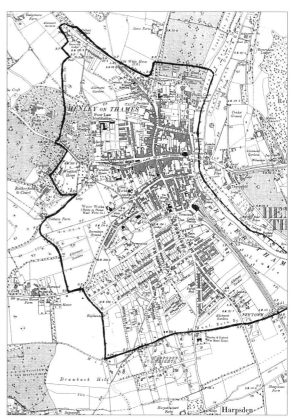

The boundaries of Henley Borough, from the Middle es till the 1800s, superimposed on an O.S. map of 1927.

56 *The boundaries of Henley Borough, from 1892 to 1932, superimposed on an O.S. map of 1927.*

their roles in public health, in road maintenance, in policing and later in education, while the parish councils had only a small impact, mainly because there was a cap on the amount of revenue they could raise through the rates. Their most important role was to induce the district and county councils to allocate resources in ways that would benefit their particular parish and, to a large extent, this remains the present situation. As a result of the re-organisation, the wide verges of the Fair Mile were transferred from Benson to Henley RDC, who continued to let them periodically for grazing.

During the 1800s, local councils gradually took over responsibility for fire fighting from the insurance companies. As part of this process, a Volunteer Fire Brigade was established in Henley in 1868, and by 1896 the brigade had 12 firemen and at least three small fire engines that were kept in the Fire Station (now an exhibition centre) in Upper Market Place.

Changes to the Town Boundary

There was a major extension of the town boundary in 1892 that took in the area of housing then being developed (in the parish of Rotherfield Greys) along the Reading and Harpsden Roads, a change that resulted in the parish of Greys losing its riverside section. The occasion was marked by a 'beating of the bounds' in which, according to the *Henley Standard*, the mayor and councillors took part in a rather spirited tour of the town boundary. This involved them in climbing fences where necessary, in being rowed along the river, and in being 'bumped' and bombarded with flour and water by local residents along the way. An extension of the boundary westwards was also proposed at about this time, but this was successfully opposed by Colonel Makins of Rotherfield Court, who objected to the increase in his rates that would have occurred if his house had been in the town rather than the rural parish of Greys.

Later, the Corporation installed marker posts, dated 1908, at various points around the boundary and some of these were moved in 1932 to reflect another extension of the boundary. Not all that are shown on the current Ordnance Survey map of the area are now visible, some presumably having been covered over by soil or rubble.

Maintaining Law and Order

In the 1830s, the Oxfordshire Justices appointed Superintending Constables who were paid a salary to supervise the local parish constables, and the one for Henley District was provided with 'staff, cutlass, handcuffs, leg irons, lantern and a rug'. In 1838, the police force in the town consisted of two parish constables appointed by the magistrates, and four manor constables appointed by the lord of the manor. The County Police Act of 1839 gave the Justices the option of setting up a fully paid police force if they wished to do so, but in Oxfordshire this was delayed until 1857 when it became compulsory. The formation of the Oxfordshire Constabulary then resulted in a police station being set up in Henley, at first in rented premises and later in a purpose-built station at the corner of Kings Road and Market Place completed in 1868. The station was enlarged in the 1890s, partly rebuilt in 1913, and used until 2005 when the police moved to more modern premises in Greys Road.

In 1869, the police force in Henley comprised a superintendent, a sergeant and one constable, but by 1881 the number of constables had been increased to three. By 1896, the officers based at Henley were a superintendent, an inspector, two sergeants and 14 constables.

Punishments for minor crime were still severe in the early 1900s. The *Henley Standard* reported in 1906 that two 'deaf mutes' were sentenced to a month's imprisonment with hard labour for not returning a costermonger's barrow, worth 10s., that they had hired from a Mr A. H. Simmons for 4d. a day.

The Disposal of Rubbish

Until the 1800s, domestic refuse was disposed of by individual households, either by burying it or composting it in their gardens, or by dumping it in the street. Most refuse, apart from glass bottles and cinders, would decompose. Following the introduction of the Public Health Act of 1875, local councils were encouraged to organise a regular collection of refuse in towns, a procedure generally known as scavenging. This was usually carried out by private contractors paid by those householders who made use of the service. Henley's rubbish was disposed of in a number of pits around the town, for example off Greys Road, the Fair Mile and at the end of Lambridge Wood Road, some of which had provided gravel for previous construction work and road improvements. In most of the villages around Henley, a major aim of the parish councils was to keep the rates to a minimum and so they failed to introduce collection schemes in response to the 1875 Act. This policy resulted in refuse and litter being dumped at the roadsides, and in increasing amounts after rubbish from newspapers, tin cans and bottles became more widespread in the years following the First World War. Henley Rural District Council finally introduced a weekly collection of household waste in the villages in 1932, and buried it in pits that had been dug in earlier years to extract chalk or clay.

Henley Town Council constructed a sewage farm near Middle Assendon in 1860 on land donated by Mr MacKenzie of Fawley Court, and this was in use till the mid-1960s when a new sewage works was built by the Marlow Road.

57   *One of the boundary posts installed around the Borough boundary in 1908: this one is in Pack and Prime Lane. (Photograph, 2006)*

The Beginning of Town Planning

Except in cities, there was little control over building until the late 1800s and the first regulations to be introduced were concerned with the structural quality of the buildings rather than their location. Increasing numbers of cheap but poor quality houses were being built during the 1800s, and local bye-laws were therefore introduced to ensure that minimum standards were met. Henley Council had formed a planning committee by the early 1880s, which insisted on compliance with the building bye-laws and also examined the plans for new buildings in the town. However, the Rural District did not adopt bye-laws of this type until 1903. They gave the councils the authority to control standards of building and the width of new streets and ensure the provision of effective sewerage. There was some control over the siting of buildings but, in Henley at least, this was applied rather inconsistently, possibly because several members of the Council were themselves builders. The lack of effective planning in Henley in about 1900 is illustrated by a situation that arose in the Norman Avenue/Albert Road area, where two builders were in competition. Charles Clements was building large detached houses in Norman Avenue and he decided to prevent a link with William Hamilton's Albert Road by building across the proposed extension of Albert Road while Hamilton was visiting North America.

6

Life in Victorian and Edwardian Henley

Social Conditions and Activities

During the reigns of Queen Victoria and King Edward VII, the livelihood of many Henley people depended, either directly or indirectly, on the nearby country houses and their estates. The houses of Park Place, Greenlands, Fawley Court and Crowsley Park were, as described in Chapter 10, all privately owned by wealthy individuals who could employ considerable numbers of domestic staff, gardeners and estate workers. Some new large houses were also constructed during this time, such as Rotherfield Court, built for the Revd Dr Morell who was Henley's rector at the time, and Friar Park, built for Frank Crisp. For most of the townspeople, life was less salubrious, as indicated by the comments made by Mr Anker Simmons, describing Henley at the time he arrived in the town in 1869: 'There was no water supply – everyone pumped water from their own well – scarcely a house in the town possessed a bathroom, and the nightly rumble of the sewage carts, a source of annoyance to light sleepers, was a reminder of the cess-pit system of drainage.' Heating and cooking involved burning wood or coal, and lighting was provided by oil lamps or candles. By 1858, most of the charities that had been set up by various individuals for the benefit of Henley were under the management of the Corporation and an account of each of them was written by John Cooper, the Town Clerk at that time.

There was considerable unemployment in the area during the early 1900s, and men from Henley would often walk to one of the surrounding farms in search of a day's work. Winter was the worst time, partly due to the lack of farm work and partly because some of the country house owners moved temporarily to their London houses, thus reducing trade and employment opportunities. Rural activities were still important in Henley's economy, and the annual Horse and Agricultural Show was held in the Market Place and Hart Street, which were closed to traffic on that day. The area around Henley was also used for troop manoeuvres and, as a result, shopkeepers in the town had their trade boosted from time to time. In September 1905, the *Henley Standard* reported that cavalry and engineers would be stationed at Danesfield, Fawley and Greenlands, while a large number of other troops would also be camped near Henley, all requiring supplies of bread and other provisions.

By the late 1800s, people with a reasonable income had increased opportunity to take part in leisure activities through sports and social clubs, many of which were church-based. In 1896 the clubs included the Church Institute Athletic Club, the Henley and District Horticultural Society, the Pleasant Sunday Afternoon Society, the Church of England Juvenile Society and the Church Lads Brigade. Henley's first cinema, the Henley Picture Palace, opened in 1911 and continued until 1935. The Picture Palace was in Bell

58 *Henley on a busy day, c.1905.*

59 *Henley Picture Palace in Bell Street, the predecessor of the Regal. (Photographed c.1930)*

Street (just south of where Waitrose now is) and, as well as showing films, was used for roller skating on Saturday afternoons and organ concerts on Sunday afternoons.

A local newspaper, the *Henley Advertiser*, was started in 1870 by a Mr Kinch who was a stationer, chemist and wine merchant, and who had, with a Mr Hickman, published a *Guide to Henley-on-Thames* in 1838. He issued the *Henley Advertiser* weekly until 1877, when it was taken over by a Mr Awbery, a supporter of the Conservative Party. The *Advertiser* was eventually forced to close by the success of its competitor, the *Henley Standard*, which had been started as the *Henley Free Press* in 1883 by the Revd Joseph Goadby. He was the minister of the Congregational Church and also a supporter of the Liberal Party, and he aimed to provide an accurate weekly account of local events. One report by the *Henley Free Press* in February 1891 noted that ice on the Thames was nine inches thick and that 'skaters have sped from Hobbs' boathouse to Regatta Island and from Marsh Lock to Shiplake'. The *Free Press* changed its name to the *Henley and South Oxfordshire Standard* in 1892, after being purchased by Archibald Brakspear and given the remit 'to assist and forward the Conservative and Unionist cause in South

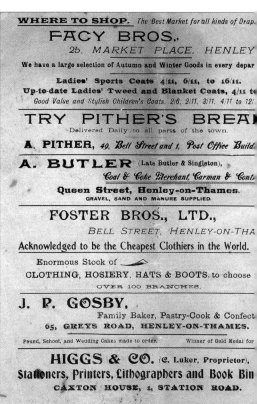

60   *The Revd Joseph Goadby who, in 1883, founded the* Henley Free Press *which later became the* Henley Standard.

61   *Advertisements for Henley businesses in the Holy Trinity parish magazine of 1913.*

62   *Skaters on the river at Henley in 1895.*

63   Advertisement for the Solomons Hatch bathing area on the Wargrave road.

HENLEY SWIMMING BATHS,
SOLOMON'S HATCH,
Are now open for Public use, daily from 6 a.m. to 8 p.m.

First-class (dressing boxes)	....	Season 21/-	.....	Month 7/6	..... Single 6d.
Second-class (covered seats)	....	,, 8/-	.....	,, 2/6	... ',, 2d.

Book containing 20 First-class Tickets, 7/6. Book containing 20 Second-class Tickets, 2/6.

The Baths are reserved for the use of Ladies, 11 a.m. to 1 p.m.,
Admission 6d. each Bath.

An experienced Swimmer and competent Teacher in constant attendance. Bathing requisites at a charge of one halfpenny for each article.

ALFRED   HASLAM, Lessee.

Oxfordshire and encourage the habits of thrift and friendly action'. In its early years the *Standard* included national as well as local news, together with sections headed 'Garden Gossip', 'Home Hints' and 'Humour of the Week'. The contract for printing it was gained by Thomas Octavius Higgs, who had set up his business on the corner of Reading Road and Station Road, where the firm of Higgs and Co. still operates. Later, Higgs and Co. was bought by Charles Luker, who in 1919 also took on ownership of the *Henley Standard*. He ran the business successfully until 1945.

An annual event that was held for some years during the 1800s was described by G.D. Leslie in 1888:

> On the fifth of November the watermen get up a subscription for a nautical Guy Fawkes. A very grotesque figure of some objectionable character is dressed up and trimmed for conflagration; he is moored on the river in an old boat and set fire to, and illumines the bank on either side.

G.D. Leslie also commented that the Solomon's Hatch bathing place, off the Wargrave Road, was 'a capital institution for Henley … The water is clear and the bottom sandy'. He noted that the bathing place was separated from the main stream of the river by a long eyot (the island now known as Rod Eyot), and that the period between 11 and 1 each day was reserved for ladies only.

Queen Victoria's Diamond Jubilee was celebrated in 1897, and to mark the event there were various parades through the town followed by a bonfire on the Mount. Higgs & Co. published an illustrated record of the Queen's reign, and the Town Council decided that the Jubilee should be commemorated by the building of a new Town Hall. It is thought that as another mark of this occasion, William MacKenzie, the owner of Henley Park and an Admiral of the Fleet, planted the group of oak trees in the shape of a Maltese Cross that still exists in the park. Various suggestions have been made as to the origin of the group of oak trees, but this is the most likely explanation. A planting date of 1897 is consistent with the fact that, although the trees appear to be more than 100 years old, they are not mentioned in Climenson's book of 1896, despite her describing the footpath route over the Mount. The trees were planted across the line of the footpath and, at the centre of the cross, the eight lines of (originally) four trees radiating from the centre are positioned so that the trunk of the closest tree of each line hides the other trunks behind it. This arrangement is still clear, though some of the trees have been lost during the intervening years.

64   *Lucy Cooper watercolour painting of the old Town Hall and Market Place, c.1890.*

65   *Lucy Cooper watercolour painting of the Thames at Henley, c.1900.*

By the early 1900s, social and political change was in the air. The Liberal Party won a national election for the first time in 1906 and the suffragette movement was gaining ground. Even in the conservative climate of Henley in 1909, suffragette speakers attracted a large crowd to a meeting in front of the Town Hall.

Help for the Poor

An infirmary for sick inmates was added to the workhouse in 1841 but life there was still tough. Jobs allocated at this time included road-mending, picking stones from the fields and the preparation of food. It is reported that the Master complained of the lack of lock-up cells for unruly paupers and that, on two occasions in May 1849, he had to remove dead bodies from the only available lock-up and place 'refractory paupers therein, in order to prevent tumult and destruction of the Union's property'. As well as housing the poorest members of the local community, the workhouse also provided temporary accommodation for the tramps who travelled across the countryside looking for casual work. Inmates who were able-bodied were forced to work hard, and some of them considered conditions in prison to be preferable to conditions in the workhouse. From time to time, they caused deliberate damage in the hope, not always fulfilled, of being sent to gaol. Despite its problems, J. S. Burn wrote in 1861 that the Henley workhouse 'has the reputation of being one of the best regulated, cleanly and orderly establishments of the kind in England'. Children living in the workhouse, who were usually either orphaned or abandoned, had to learn a trade and had also to receive instruction from a chaplain. By the mid-1890s, the workhouse was accomodating about forty tramps each night. In 1905, the *Henley Standard* reported that a tramp was sentenced to 21 days' hard labour for denying, when he claimed admittance, that he had any money or food with him whereas, on being searched the next morning, he was found to have 16d. in his bundle of belongings. John Crocker, who died aged 99 in 2004, remembered as a boy seeing the inmates of the workhouse returning from church, the women in long striped dresses from neck to ankle and the men in grey suits. He also noted that his grandfather resigned from

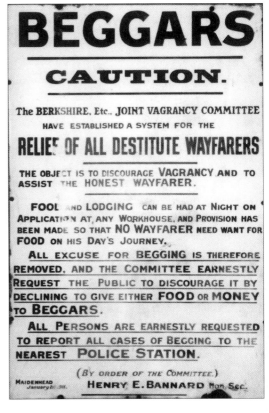

66 *A notice to beggars erected in Henley in 1911 (now in the lobby of the Hart Surgery).*

the Town Council in protest at what he considered to be inhuman conditions at the workhouse. In an attempt to prevent begging, a notice was erected in the town in 1911 by the Berks, Bucks and Oxon Joint Vagrancy Committee warning the public not to offer food and drink to beggars, who could obtain a meal at the workhouse. Any occurrence of begging was to be reported to the Police Station.

For poor people who had homes, such as those elderly without the support of a family or an ex-employer, the Relieving Officer could recommend the Poor Law Guardians to provide 'outdoor relief'. However, this was little more than enough to prevent starvation. It was only in 1909, when the government introduced a modest Old Age Pension for those over 70, funded by taxation, that poor elderly people had some basic security. The pension resulted in a large decline in the number of people living in the workhouse and also in those who received 'outdoor relief'.

According to the parish magazine of St Mary's Church, a Henley Work Society had been established in 1853 in order to 'render assistance to poor and deserving women by supplying them at their own homes with needlework, consisting principally of articles of clothing which are afterwards sold to the poor at nearly the cost of the materials'. It was funded by voluntary contributions from the parishioners.

The poorest and generally least law-abiding area of Henley appears to have been in and around West Street, and policemen venturing there went in pairs.

Improvements in Medical Provision

Infectious diseases, such as scarlet fever, diphtheria, tuberculosis and smallpox, were a major concern during the Victorian period, and the Public Health Act of 1848 drew attention to the factors that might be responsible for the spread of such diseases. Towns were required to establish Local Boards of Health to examine and deal with the hazards that might arise from shortcomings in the water supply, sewerage and street cleaning services, and in the location of slaughter houses. A Sanitary Inspector for Henley was appointed in 1856 but the appointment appears to have been a part-time one. His main responsibility was to prevent any outbreak of a serious infectious disease from spreading, and the recommended policy was for the patient to be isolated so far as possible. In Henley Rural District, a Sanitary Authority was created in 1872 simply by renaming the Henley Union's Board of Guardians. The policy of isolating patients with infectious diseases was promoted some years later by W.H. Smith and his son, Viscount Hambleden, who paid for the construction of a district isolation hospital, known as the Smith Hospital, at the end of the Fair Mile. The hospital project was also supported by Mr W.D. MacKenzie of Fawley Court, who donated the land on which it was built. The hospital was passed to the Rural District Sanitary Authority in 1892 and was fitted out with the latest equipment and furnishings. While no charge was made to 'working class' patients, others had to pay up to £5 5s. per week for their stay.

General medical practice developed during the early 1900s with the roles of GP, physician and surgeon becoming increasingly distinct, and the physicians and surgeons being based in the larger hospitals. Nursing also became more professional, and in 1908 the Oxfordshire County Nursing Federation was formed with responsibilities for training and supervision. When the National Insurance Act was introduced in 1911, all working men became eligible to be placed on the 'panel' of a GP, who was then paid an annual fee to provide their general medical care. The Ministry of Health was created in 1919, and soon afterwards the concept of a National Health Service was being considered, though it was nearly thirty years before it was implemented.

School Expansion

The Victorian period was marked by new school building. The National School that had already been established in rented premises in New Street was replaced in 1856 by a newly-built school, with separate sections for boys, girls and infants, on a site on the south side of Gravel Hill. This new school could accommodate 520 children and was supported partly by fees and partly by grants from the Council of Education, the National Society and the Oxford Diocesan Board. It also incorporated two sets of apartments, for the headmaster and headmistress. The school had a large garden which was cultivated by the boys, partly as a means of fitting them for employment as gardeners. After about 1860, girls were also taught vocational skills:

> washing, ironing, cooking and other useful employments to qualify them as domestic servants and as thrifty wives for the labouring classes!

The British school that had been established in rented premises by the Congregational Church was replaced in 1856 by a newly built school on the corner of Reading Road and Norman Avenue. In 1860 it had 85 pupils, both boys and girls, and was supported partly by the fees of pupils and partly by funding from the British Society. From 1871, it received a government grant. However, the school closed in 1932, largely due to the high costs of maintenance.

In 1861 a night school was opened at the National School on two evenings a week during the winter, to teach men and boys above the age of 16 to read and write. These adult pupils were not charged for their tuition but they had to provide their own copybooks. The main instructor was one of the curates and he was assisted by two or three parishioners.

The building of both the British and National Schools in Henley would have been eligible for funds from the government as, in 1833, Parliament had authorised such support on condition that matching funds were forthcoming. The government took a more direct role in education from 1862, when annual grants were made to schools on the basis of the number of pupils taught by certificated teachers, together with the results of an annual examination conducted by Her Majesty's Inspectors. A major aim of the Education Act of 1870 was to provide schools for all children, and where voluntary schools were unable to meet the need School Boards were to be set up in order to provide Board schools. None was needed in Henley. In 1880, school attendance was made compulsory and in 1899 the leaving age was specified as twelve.

Truancy was punished. The *Henley Standard* reported in 1897 that a boy was sentenced to six strokes of the birch from a police sergeant for persistent truancy despite being sent to school by his mother. Although the Education Act stipulated that 'no child was to be compelled to attend religious instruction in any elementary school', the influence of religion was still important. The Grammar School (not an elementary school) in Henley was dominated by the Church of England to the extent that children of nonconformist families were threatened with expulsion if they did not attend the parish church on Sundays. Under the headship of a Revd Godby in the mid-1800s, the Grammar School expanded to include, as well as local boys, more than 50 who boarded in a house adjoining the school.

As Henley's population grew, school provision expanded. A new church school was built by Trinity Church in Greys Hill in 1893, and a schoolroom for infants was added to the rear of the British School in 1901. Under the Education Act of 1902, county and borough councils were given the responsibility of acting as Local Education Authorities, able to use some of their rate income to make grants to all publicly-funded schools, especially church schools. By this time there were several good private schools in the Henley area, together with the Catholic Sacred Heart School which had opened in 1894.

In 1841 the United Charity Schools, comprising the Grammar and Periam Schools, moved to rooms at the *Bell Inn*, where trade was beginning to decline. The Bell eventually closed completely and was bought at auction in 1853 by Edward MacKenzie with the rest of the Fawley estate. Mr Mackenzie continued to let part of the premises at the *Bell* for use by the schools. The two schools were merged in 1892 by the Charity Commissioners and became known as Henley Grammar School, which then had 20 non-paying pupils and 35 who paid fees of £3 a year. After 1902, the school received a grant from the County Council and it continued at the *Bell* until 1928, when it moved to Rotherfield Court and the *Bell* was divided into private houses, as it is now.

The Henley-on-Thames School of Science and Art was established in 1873, its main role being to provide evening classes for adults. At first it was in Hart Street and later in Duke Street.

67 The Grammar School in premises at the old Bell Inn at Northfield End, late 1800s.

Churches and Chapels

The interior of St Mary's Church was refurbished and modified in 1852, giving it a Victorian appearance which, to some extent, has been retained. Box pews and galleries that had been added in 1818 were removed, some new windows were added and an organ installed. While the church was being renovated, services were held in what is now the Kenton Theatre. In 1868 one of the turrets on the tower was struck by lightning and fell onto the roof, causing considerable damage. All the stained glass windows were installed after the refurbishment of 1852, many of them donated in the early 1900s by Sir William Makins of Rotherfield Court in memory of his family or friends.

By the mid-1800s, when Henley was expanding beyond the town's boundary into Rotherfield Greys parish, a new church, Holy Trinity, was built to meet the changing needs of the area. A building fund was established and this enabled the church, in flint and stone, to be built in Greys Hill in 1848. A new ecclesiastical parish was then formed out of portions of Rotherfield Greys, Rotherfield Peppard and Henley. The church was enlarged in 1891, with donations from W.H. Smith and John Noble among others, and the area of the churchyard was greatly increased by a donation of land from the vicar. The gates that are now at the main entrance to the churchyard in Greys Hill once formed the entrance to Henley Town Hall, and were removed from there in 1909 when they were replaced by oak doors.

The Independent Meeting House in Reading Road had been enlarged in 1829 and became the home of the Congregationalists. The present Christ Church building was constructed nearby in 1908, with Sir Frank Crisp of Friar Park paying for the tower and steeple, as indicated by an inscription at its base. After the completion of Christ Church, the Meeting House, which was by the roadside and nearer to the Manse, was demolished. Christ Church continued as the home of the Congregationalists and, since 1972, of the United Reform Church. The building was extended in 2000 to accommodate the Christ Church Centre, which is now a venue for various meetings and events.

In 1896 there were, in addition, other churches or chapels in Henley, run by the Roman Catholics in Station Road, the Wesleyans in Duke Street, the Baptists in Market Place, the Strict Baptists in Gravel Hill, and the Quakers in Northfield End. The Baptists

68   Christ Church soon after its construction in 1908.

and the Quakers continue to use the premises that were in use in 1896, the Quaker Meeting House having been rebuilt in 1894.

Arrival of the Railway

The first proposal for a railway to come to Henley was for a line to run from Tring to Basingstoke via Henley and Reading. It was proposed that the track would reach Assendon through a tunnel and approach Henley alongside the Fair Mile. Fortunately this suggestion did not materialise. In 1840-1, the Great Western Railway (GWR) opened the line from Paddington to Reading and Bristol, and a horse-drawn coach service was quickly introduced to take passengers between Henley and the nearest station at Twyford. Although a branch railway line to Henley was authorised in 1847, work was delayed until the mid-1850s due to a shortage of funds and discussions over various alternative plans. Local residents had agreed to subscribe £15,000 towards the cost, which was estimated at £45,000 though, in fact, the total cost came to £79,000, of which the Henley townspeople managed to raise only £9,500.

The branch line finally opened in 1857 as a broad-gauge single track, and the event was celebrated by a public breakfast at the Town Hall. Laying the track was comparatively easy, apart from two bridges over the Thames which, initially, were of wooden trestle construction and limited the speed of trains to 20 m.p.h. The track crossed Mill Lane by a level crossing, and the crossing-keeper's cottage is still there, though considerably enlarged, close to the embankment that now leads to the bridge over that track. The branch line ended at the south-east edge of the town, and so both it and the station were constructed without any buildings having to be demolished. Station Road was built by the GWR specifically to provide access to the station and, until 1877, belonged to the railway company, who closed access to it every evening.

Conversion of the broad gauge track to standard gauge was carried out in 1876, the Henley branch being the last of all the lines owned by the GWR to be converted. In 1891, the platforms at Henley station were extended, primarily to cope with the crowds attracted to the Regatta and, a few years later, the railway was widened from single to double track. In addition, the wooden bridges over the river were replaced by iron girders and the level crossing at Mill Lane was replaced by a bridge. In 1897, the GWR put forward plans to connect the Henley and Marlow branch lines by building a bridge over the river and taking the track along part of the Regatta course, but this scheme was dropped thanks to 'enormous public opposition'.

Initially the only intermediate station on the Henley branch was at Shiplake but a second station at Wargrave was opened in 1900. There was a circular turntable for engines at Henley station, originally to the north of the platforms, which accounts for the crescent-shaped bend by Perpetual House in Station Road. The bend became unnecessary when a new turntable was built, in 1903-4, on the land now occupied by Hewgate Court, and a straight section of road was introduced by the station entrance. As well as serving commuters, the railway soon became an important means of delivering goods to the town. Large amounts of coal were brought in, partly for use on household fires and partly for the gas works and other local industries. The coal was stored temporarily in a coal yard next to the station on the east side, and there was a goods depot on the west side, together with the turntable, according to a 1897 plan of the station layout.

By 1900, commuters from Henley had a reliable train service and, although most of the passenger trains to Paddington took more than an hour, two direct trains per day took only 50 minutes. This encouraged more commuters to move to Henley, and the station was enlarged to provide a new booking hall in 1904.

Problems on the Roads

Once the railways from London were opened in the mid-1800s, long-distance travel on horseback or by horse-drawn coach quickly diminished. Many turnpike trusts failed to attract any bids for the right to collect tolls, and soon ceased to operate. For example, the Henley-Dorchester Turnpike Trust was wound up in 1873, and the toll house at Bix was then sold for £75. When a trust ceased to operate, any remaining funds were divided

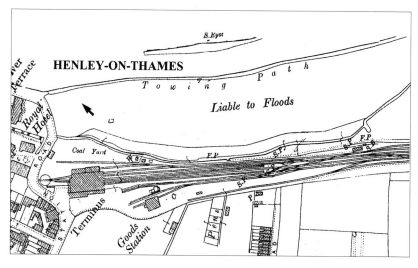

69   *A plan of Henley railway station, 1897.*

70 *Henley railway station from Station Road, c.1910.*

amongst the appropriate parishes, which then resumed their liability for road repairs. However, the condition of the roads deteriorated and so, when the responsibility for maintaining the turnpiked roads was transferred to the newly formed county councils in 1888, there was soon pressure from the public for road maintenance to be improved. Responsibility for roads that had not been turnpiked remained with the local highways boards, such as the Henley Highways Board, but their responsibilities were passed to the district councils by the Local Government Act of 1894.

Steam engines, as well as pulling trains, were also used as traction engines for pulling heavy loads on the roads. Building materials, such as bricks and tiles from Nettlebed, timber from sawmills, such as the one at Middle Assendon, and also crops from farms were often transported in this way, and a notice was erected on each corner of Henley bridge warning engine drivers that only one loaded truck should be taken over the bridge at one time. These notices are still in place.

When cycling became popular, the campaign for better road surfaces received extra support. Bicycles with pneumatic tyres came on the scene in the 1870s, and cycling soon became widely adopted both for pleasure and for journeys to and from work. In 1876 an article appeared in the *St Mary's Parish Magazine* extolling this new trend:

> It is scarcely ten years ago that the era of bicycling commenced and that the first machine, a wooden one, was imported from Paris … We now have elegant machines of a height and lightness, and capable of being propelled at a speed undreamt of by the most enthusiastic bicyclist of 10 years ago … Bicycles were but lately objects of most bitter hatred and disgust with some people, and their speedy extinction was loudly prophesied but they seem to have outraced all the silly objections that were once thrown at them and now hold their place as a well established means of travel.

By 1896, there were three cycling clubs in Henley: the up-market Henley Cycling Club, the Henley Wheelers Cycling Club for 'young working men' and a branch of the Cyclist Touring Club. In the campaign for better road surfaces, the cyclists were soon joined by motorists, who also suffered from frequent punctures, as well as from dust if two or more vehicles were travelling together. Initially the speed of motor vehicles was restricted to four m.p.h. but it

71   *A steam traction engine used by Brakspear's Brewery.*

72   *A coach building firm in Northfield End that took the opportunity of diversifying to include garage facilities for motor vehicles, c.1905. The cedar of Lebanon survived until December 1981 when it succumbed to an exceptional snowfall.*

was raised to 14 m.p.h. in 1896, and to 20 m.p.h. in 1903, though a local authority could impose a limit of 10 m.p.h. on some roads if this was considered necessary.

Rough road surfaces were a problem not only for cyclists and motorists but also for people living in houses near the roadsides. In July 1905, a resident of Reading Road in Henley complained that 'The dust from the motor traffic last Sunday was unbearable. Not a window could be opened and one could hardly see across the road.' In the town, the dust was sometimes reduced by using a water cart to moisten the road surfaces, but

73 *An early motor bus that caught fire in Henley.*

this procedure was not extended to the surrounding villages, though Wargrave did invest in a water cart of its own.

Roads were still surfaced mainly with stones collected locally, and in February 1906 the *Henley Standard* reported:

> The heavy rains of last week have had one good effect in that they have proved how utterly unsuitable flint is for the making of highway roads and it is with pleasure that all road users of the Nettlebed-Henley road have noted that, in future, granite is to be used instead of the wretched flint which, if cheaper to buy, is dearer in the long run, not to mention the damage it does to the rubber tyres of the motor-car, the bicycle and the carriage. It is probably a long time since the road from Henley to Nettlebed was in so bad a state as at present.

Boats for Commerce and Pleasure

Barge transport on rivers and canals received a set-back from the new railways, and the Thames Commissioners were amongst those who had opposed the construction of the Great Western Railway. However, although the railways competed with the rivers for transporting heavy loads, the effect on the barge owners was partly offset by the increase in demand that resulted from the ongoing industrial revolution. The Thames Conservancy was formed in 1857 with responsibility for the whole of the river between London and Cricklade, and it soon organised the rebuilding and strengthening of many of the locks built in the 1770s. Marsh Lock was rebuilt in 1883. Dredging was also introduced on a regular basis, and in the late 1800s steam barges and steam tugs began to appear as replacements for horses. The end of the horse era was regretted by some, including Emily Climenson, who wrote: 'these picturesque craft are rapidly disappearing, transmogrified into ugly steam tugs'.

By the 1870s, the railways actually began to bring a new source of income for the Thames Conservancy in the form of tourism. In Henley, as in other towns such as Marlow and Maidenhead, there were numerous visitors from London who arrived by train, some for a day-trip, some for a longer stay, and many of them spent time on a boat on the river. By 1887, the tolls collected at the locks from pleasure boats were about three times more than those from barges. Visitors to Henley were most numerous at Regatta time when there were hundreds of pleasure boats, of all sizes, on the river.

Petrol-powered boats started to appear in the early 1900s and, in response to concerns about their safety, the Thames Conservancy introduced a new regulation that prohibited any such boat from entering a lock in which other craft were present. According to the *Henley Standard*, this was 'to prevent a panic that might otherwise occur as the result of a boat of the description mentioned bursting into flame'.

As cars and motorcycles became more affordable during the end of the Edwardian period, they were seen as a new threat to the boating trade. One owner of a boat-hiring business is reported to have commented, 'Why, there are even girls who'll hang on the back of a motorbike instead of making themselves comfortable in one of my punts.'

Henley Royal Regatta

The first Oxford and Cambridge boat race took place in 1829 on a course from Hambleden to Henley, and this provided the inspiration for the first Henley Regatta. The University Boat Race took place again on this course in 1837, and attracted numerous visitors to the town. Henley traders welcomed them and the supporters of both crews congregated at the *Red Lion*. The rowing fraternity expressed a particular interest in the relatively wide and nearly straight section of the river between Henley Bridge and Temple Island, a distance of about one and a half miles, the longest stretch of straight water on the non-tidal Thames, and so a committee was formed to organise a Regatta to be held over this course in 1839. It was decided that races should be rowed against the flow of the river so that Henley's inns and shops would be readily accessible to the spectators, most of whom would be near the finish.

Six stewards were appointed, including Thomas Stonor of Stonor Park, William Fuller-Maitland of Park Place, William Freeman of Fawley Court and Charles Lane of Badgemore (plus Edmund Gardiner and the mayor), and funds were raised to purchase the Grand Challenge Cup, costing £105, and the Town Challenge Cup, costing £31. Another effect of the interest in rowing was that the Henley Rowing Club was formed in the same year, 1839. The first Regatta occupied a single afternoon and had just three events, the Grand Challenge Cup being awarded for eights and the Town Challenge Cup for fours. There were four entries for the Grand Challenge Cup, three from Oxford colleges and one from Cambridge. In the following year, many other rowing clubs, including the Leander, applied to enter the Regatta, and the racing was therefore extended to two days. And Leander won the Grand Challenge Cup.

The Earl of Macclesfield was the patron for the first four Regattas and he was succeeded by Lord Camoys, who continued as patron until Prince Albert accepted the role in 1851. It then became known as the Henley Royal Regatta. The popularity of the Regatta had declined to some extent, partly due to competition from other regattas at Maidenhead and Marlow, but it was revived by the royal patronage and, a few years later, by the opening of the railway. After the death of Prince Albert, Queen Victoria took over the position of patron.

The Regatta was one of the major social occasions in England from about 1870 until the First World War and, during this period, attracted large numbers of visitors. Until 1885, a grandstand for spectators was put up on the roadway in front of the *Red Lion Hotel*. Each year, the river was crowded by pleasure boats, and in 1885 there were more than 100 houseboats and nearly 1,500 rowing boats of various types. The more elaborate houseboats were 'furnished with profuse magnificence, with refrigerators, pianos etc,

74 *The first Oxford &*
Cambridge Boat Race, held at
Henley, on 10 June 1829.

75 *A poster for the second*
day of Henley Regatta in 1845,
listing the crews competing in
seven events.

SECOND DAY.

HENLEY GRAND REGATTA,
SATURDAY JUNE 7th. 1845.

THE RACE FOR

THE GRAND CHALLENGE CUP,

Will take place at Two o'Clock precisely.

OXFORD—UNIVERSITY BOAT CLUB - - - - - *Purple.*
CAMBRIDGE—UNIVERSITY BOAT CLUB- - - - *Light Blue.*

THE DISTRICT CHALLENGE CUP,

WINDSOR—WINDSOR & ETON BOAT CLUB - - - *Light Blue and White*
HENLEY—AQUATIC CLUB - - - - - - - - - *Light Blue.*

A London Waterman's Match.

THE DIAMOND SCULLS,

LONDON—H. CHAPMAN—CRESCENT CLUB- - No. 2. *Yellow.*
OXFORD—J. W. CONANT—ST. JOHN'S - - - No. 4. *Dark Blue.*
LONDON—S. WALLACE—LEANDER CLUB - - No. 6. *Green.*

THE NEW CHALLENGE CUP,

CAMBRIDGE—THE BLACK PRINCE - - - - - *Purple.*
CAMBRIDGE—THE LADY MARGARET - - - - *Red.*
LONDON—ST. GEORGE'S CLUB - - - - - - *White, Red Cross.*

THE TOWN CHALLENGE CUP,

HENLEY—AQUATIC CLUB - - - - - - - - *Light Blue.*
HENLEY—DREADNOUGHT CUTTER CLUB - - - - *Withdrawn*

THE SILVER WHERRIES,

LONDON—E. G. PEACOCK } AMATEUR SCULLERS CLUB } No.1 *Light Blue*
—H. CHAPMAN } CRESCENT CLUB - - - }

CAMBRIDGE —ARNOLD } CAIUS COLLEGE No. 4 *Light Blue & White*
—MANN }

THE STEWARDS CHALLENGE CUP,

OXFORD—UNIVERSITY BOAT CLUB *(The Holders)* *Dark Blue.*
LONDON—ST. GEORGE'S CLUB - - - - - - *White, Red Cross.*

SIGNALS:

The 1st GUN AT ½-PAST One For Boats to drop to Stations and clear the Course
„ 2nd GUN - - - - - That the course is clear.
„ 3rd GUN AT THE ISLAND To Start.
„ 4th GUN - - - That the race is ended.
☞ The COLOURS refer to the small Flags in he Bows of the Racing Boats.

The Races will follow at intervals of half an hour.

Printed by HICKMAN & KINCH, Post-Office, Henley,

NOTICE.

Great inconvenience was yesterday experienced by the Crews from SAILING BOATS and STEAM YACHTS Sailing and Steaming on the Regatta Course during the time of the Races,

The Stewards therefore urgently request that Gentlemen in command of Yachts and Boats will abstain from accompanying the Races and from intruding on the Course.

CHARLES TOWSEY,
Secretary.

Committee Room,
THURSDAY, 29th JUNE, 1865.

E. KINCH, PRINTER, HENLEY.

76   *A notice issued during the Regatta of 1865 designed to keep the course clear of spectators' boats.*

with kitchens in a separate boat and a host of attendant servants'. Other spectators crowded the riverbanks but, according to a magazine article, 'The crowds do not come here to see at all. They come to be seen. It is a society show.' In 1888, 6,768 people travelled by train from London to Henley on the second day of the Regatta, while in 1895 an average of 11,380 people came on each day of the Regatta, which by then lasted for three days. And, as the Regatta was held during the middle of the week, most of the spectators were from wealthy backgrounds.

Originally the course ran from Temple Island to a finishing line by the *Red Lion* but, because this involved a slight bend in the course at Poplar Point (now no longer with its poplar trees, the last one being felled in 1983), it gave boats on the Berkshire side a potential advantage. Although this advantage was often offset by the wind, as the Bucks side was more sheltered, it was decided in 1886 to move the finishing line to Poplar Point and the start line a little further downstream. Also from that year, wooden booms were fixed alongside the course to keep it clear of spectators' boats which had been liable to obstruct the rowers. Until 1893, swans on the river were also liable to disrupt the races and, as it was impossible to keep them away from the course temporarily, it was decided to catch them and move them away from Henley for the whole Regatta period. In more recent years they have been caught and taken by road to the Egham Swan Sanctuary, the Regatta stewards paying the cost of the move.

By 1906, the increasing popularity of the Regatta had resulted in it being extended to four days. The Phyllis Court Club had just opened and the *Henley Standard* reported, 'An observation taken on Henley Bridge yielded the astonishing information that over 500 cars passed in an hour. There were 200 at Phyllis Court and, all over the town, garages were full to utmost capacity.' Two years later, not only did the usual Regatta take place but Henley also hosted the rowing events of the 1908 Olympic Games. Royal support for the Regatta was continued by King George V and Queen Mary who, in 1912, were rowed along the course in a State barge and later had lunch at Greenlands, the home of Viscount Hambleden. The Stewards Enclosure opened in 1919, adding to the social cachet of the event. To improve the course for the rowers, it was straightened further in 1924 by digging away part of Temple Island and also part of the bank at Remenham. But it was still only possible for two boats to compete at the same time.

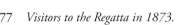

77   *Visitors to the Regatta in 1873.*

78   *A cartoon from the time of the Regatta in 1880.*

79   *Another cartoon from the time of the Regatta in 1880.*

80   *Spectators' boats at the Regatta, c.1900.*

81   *Regatta spectators at Temple Island, c.1890.*

The Leander Club was formed in London in 1818 and it dominated amateur rowing for the next twenty years. The Club did not enter the first Henley Regatta but won the Grand Challenge Cup in the second Regatta in 1840. As the Regatta became increasingly important among the rowing fraternity, Leander decided to build a new boathouse/clubhouse at Henley. It leased a site on the Remenham side of the bridge from the Henley Corporation and took over its new building in 1896. But Leander continued to regard itself as a London club, and the Henley premises, especially the bedrooms for rowers, were rather sparsely furnished. Improvements were carried out from time to time and the clubhouse building was substantially extended and modernised in 1986 and again in 1998. Some of Britain's most successful recent rowers trained at the Club, and these have included Steve Redgrave, Matthew Pinsent, James Cracknell and Tim Foster, who won the gold medal for coxless fours at the Olympics in Sydney in September 2000.

Sports and Sports Clubs in Henley

As noted earlier, the first reported team match in Henley was a game of cricket played in 1766. The Henley Cricket Club, with its ground in Remenham Lane, was in existence

82 *Regatta spectators near Phyllis Court, c.1900.*

by 1850, when it was reported that 'members have acquired considerable local celebrity in this truly English game'. Mr J.F. Hodges of Bolney Court was president at the time. Since 1850 several different cricket clubs have been formed but most have lasted for only a few years. One that survived for longer was the Henley Town Cricket Club that was formed in 1886 with a lower subscription than that of the Henley Cricket Club and with the aim of attracting a more working-class membership. By 1900, both of the two cricket clubs had grounds in Remenham Lane. Subsequently, Henley Town Cricket Club played at Station Meadow before moving to the present cricket field at the bottom of White Hill. The present Henley Cricket Club was founded in 1974 and in 2004-6 raised the funds to purchase the freehold of this field.

Henley Town Football Club was formed in 1871-2, at about the same time as the competition for the FA Cup was started. The original ground was at Dry Leas in Marlow Road, and in 1880 Henley's team contained two members of the gentry, the Hon. R. Jervis and the Hon. E.N. Rolls. In the early 1900s, there was an annual football match between a team composed of staff from Henley Station and another team from the staff of Henley Post Office.

Although Henley Grammar School was playing a game similar to rugby in 1869, it was decided in 1875 that soccer should be played, and this decision held until 1924, when rugby was played again. The present, successful, Henley Rugby Club originated in 1930 as the Old Henliensians (old boys of the Grammar School), and this was re-founded in 1954 and became Henley Rugby Football Club in 1963.

The land at Harpsden for Henley Golf Club was purchased in 1905 by a syndicate registered as Bolney Estates Ltd. A nine-hole course opened two years later and this was extended to 18 holes in 1908. A tennis club was first established in Henley in about 1884 with four courts near the junction of Marlow Road and Northfield End, but tennis in Henley has had a rather chequered history, none of the clubs that have been formed being able to acquire courts on a long-term basis. Hockey, according to John Bailey, was first played in Henley in 1881, but the present club developed from a ladies team of ex-Grammar School players who, in 1951, decided to form the Henley Hockey Club.

7

The Effects of the First World War and the 1920s

The Effects of the War in Henley

At the outbreak of the First World War in July 1914, it was generally thought that the end of the fighting would come within a few months, but it soon became clear that this view was over-optimistic. However, the combination of patriotism and the early optimism attracted many volunteers for the army in response to a government recruiting campaign. Most of those from Henley joined the Oxfordshire and Buckinghamshire Light Infantry. The troops needed horses for transport, and this need was met by requisitioning any that were not essential for civilian work, a process that was supervised in south Oxfordshire by Colonel Paul Makins of Chilterns End, Henley. There was widespread concern about possible spying by enemy agents, and unrecognised individuals in any locality were liable to be suspected. A Henley councillor, Mr J.T. Campion, was arrested while using binoculars during a holiday based at Bognor, and several phone calls between Henley and Bognor were needed before he was released. Various foreign nationals, including the manager of the *Red Lion Hotel*, who was of German parentage, were interned.

As the war progressed, the *Henley Standard* reported developments on the battlefields of France, including the deaths of local men, as well as providing its usual news of events in the Henley area. It also recorded deliberations of the Town Council aimed at encouraging recruitment to the army and discouraging people from stockpiling food. Injured soldiers began to arrive back from France and some were treated in the Town Hall, the upper floor of which was converted to a Red Cross hospital. There were 24 beds and the patients were looked after mainly by local volunteers. Other war casualties were accommodated during their convalescence by Colonel Leonard Noble of Harpsden Court.

Many members of the civilian population were affected by having relatives in the armed services and, in some instances, by the increased job opportunities available for women. Other difficulties were caused by increases in the price of food and by the loss of horses for transport. And street lighting, at that time provided by gas lamps, was reduced to lessen the risk of an air raid on the town. By the end of the war, many of the men who had joined the armed services had been killed or injured, most of them fighting in France, and the deaths of 186 men from Henley are recorded on memorial tablets on the front wall of the Town Hall.

Once the war was over, those men who did return without physical injury often found it difficult to gain employment. A combination of inflation and increased taxation had reduced the incomes of the local estate-owners, who found their previous lifestyle impossible to maintain and were unable to employ the same numbers as they did before the war. Also, in the town itself, women had taken on some of the jobs previously carried out by the men who had joined the army. In June 1918, women over the age of 31 gained the right to vote in elections and, to the surprise of some commentators, took this right

83   *A company of yeomanry leaving Henley in 1914.*

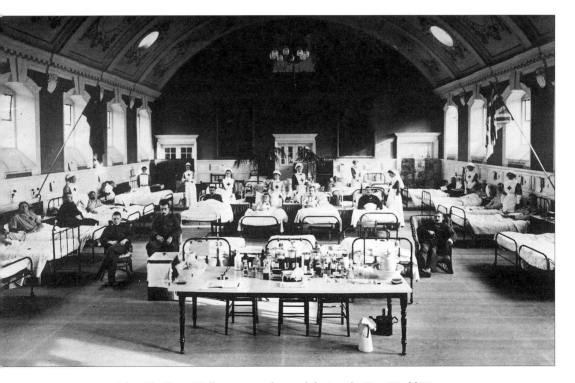

84   *The Town Hall in use as a hospital during the First World War.*

85 *The War Memorial Hospital built in Harpsden Way and opened in 1923.*

seriously. In the winter of 1918-19, the loss of life caused by the war was compounded by an influenza epidemic which affected the whole country for several months. There were scores of deaths in the Henley area, some of the local schools were closed for weeks at a time, and the Picture Palace announced that its premises were fumigated twice daily as a precaution. Despite the problems of unemployment, illness and housing shortages, some months after the war ended, the town organised a celebration of victory and the return of peace. It was held on 19 July 1919 and began with a reception for returned servicemen at the Town Hall. This was followed by processions, a fete during the afternoon at Fawley Court, and finally a bonfire on the Mount.

Although the wealthy families living at the surrounding country houses had a less opulent lifestyle than they did before 1914, they still had some household staff and were significant in the local economy. Everyone was affected by the large price increases that occurred for most items, including bread and milk and building materials, during the years 1919-21. Inflation led to cuts in government expenditure and thus contributed to a slump and a high rate of unemployment. However, the growth in the adult population resulting from the large size of many families in Victorian times, together with the lack of building during the war years, resulted in a housing shortage, and to meet the local demand the built-up area of the town expanded considerably during the 1920s. The town's first council houses were built in 1919-22 in Vicarage Road and Western Avenue, and many private houses were also built, mostly in the southern part of the town. Allotments were popular and a map of Henley issued in 1927 shows eight separate areas of 'allotment gardens' in and around the town. The town's livestock market was still held, though on a smaller scale than before 1914, and in the 1920s it was moved from the Market Place to the yard of the *White Hart*.

During the 1920s, the Chantry House was purchased from the owner of the *Red Lion Hotel* and presented to St Mary's Church, using funds that had been donated in memory of a recent rector. Some restoration work was carried out and the name Chantry House was adopted.

86   *Traffic on Henley Bridge at Regatta time during the 1920s.*

Medical Provision in the 1920s

In Henley, it was decided to build a cottage hospital as a memorial to the 339 servicemen from the town and surrounding district who had died during the war. There was a definite need for a hospital, as the senior doctor in the town had reported that he had to carry out three recent operations in private homes in unsatisfactory conditions. A committee was formed with Viscount Hambleden as president. A plot of land in Harpsden Way was donated for the hospital by the father of a soldier killed in the war, and fund-raising towards a target of £20,000 was begun. Various individuals and societies made donations, a number of events were organised to raise money, and surrounding parishes contributed to the fund. In one event, Henley residents contributed a line of coins from the Town Hall to the foundation stone. The War Memorial Hospital was finally opened with an appropriate ceremony in June 1923. A total of about £23,000 had been raised of which a little more than half was taken up by the cost of the building, and the remainder was invested to generate an income, needed for staff salaries and medical equipment. There were two public wards and three private rooms, together with an operating theatre and X-ray facilities, and these represented a major addition to medical facilities in Henley. However, long-term care continued to be provided by the infirmary at Townlands, and this role was maintained after the workhouse became a Public Assistance Institution in 1930.

Poverty in the 1920s

There were fewer poor people needing workhouse accommodation once an old age pension was introduced in 1909, and especially after the pension was doubled in 1919 and again when the pensionable age was reduced to 65 in 1925. However, the workhouse continued to provide temporary accommodation for tramps, and in 1926 there were on average 20 tramps per night staying at Townlands. In 1929, the responsibilities of Poor Law Unions with their workhouses and relieving officers were transferred to the County Councils. The Boards of Guardians were then disbanded and the workhouses renamed Public Assistance Institutions. They became, in effect, long-stay hospitals or care homes, though most kept some accommodation for tramps and unemployed people who were seeking work. Real poverty, defined as unavoidable near-starvation, had disappeared.

At a rather less serious level of deprivation, the families of people who were unemployed continued to face hardship after the end of the war. In Henley, the mayoress organised a soup kitchen for children, funded by local subscriptions, through the winter of 1921-2. It was based at the Police Station and ran for four months, attracting about 150 children every day. Even by 1925, a lack of money was still causing some people to send their children to school without shoes. Unemployment continued to be a problem in Henley until the late 1930s and groups of unemployed men often congregated in the town centre.

Changes in Schools

The school leaving age was raised from 12 to 14 in 1918 and most children left school completely at 14. By the 1920s, the National School at Gravel Hill had become a boys school, and the girls were at Trinity School in Greys Hill. The school still had its large garden, cultivated by the boys. A new Infants School was built in Greys Road in 1932, and the younger children moved there from the National Schools.

The Grammar School became a County Council School in 1928 and moved from the *Bell* to Rotherfield Court. It became co-educational at the same time, and its normal leaving age was 16. Parents of children at the Grammar School had to pay fees until the Education Act of 1944, and this forced some parents to refuse a place there, even when their child had passed the entrance exam. However, the various endowments that had supported the Grammar School and its two predecessors prior to 1928 were transferred to the trustees of the newly formed Henley Educational Charity, who used the income from their property and investments to fund a limited number of scholarships and to improve educational facilities in the town.

The First Tarmac

During the early 1900s and even in the 1920s, many roads were still surfaced with stones or gravel. Women and children from families needing cash, and inmates of the workhouse, were employed to collect stones from farmers' fields, and the stones were then sold to either the District or the County Council for use on the roads. Steam rollers were used to crush the stones and provide a reasonably smooth surface. Although a few roads were sprayed with tar or treated with 'asphaltic grouting', motor vehicles and bicycles suffered from frequent punctures. Partly for this reason, horse transport was considered as more reliable than motor transport in rural areas, at least until 1929, when the county councils took on responsibility for minor as well as major roads, and tarmac surfaces became more widespread. Even after that, horses were widely used for short journeys and for the local delivery of goods till the late 1940s, when motor vehicles became increasingly dominant.

87   *Deliveries in Bell Street by horse and cart, 1920s.*

Disruptions on the Railway

During the First World War, the government took over all the railways in the country and government traffic, such as the transport of troops and military equipment, took precedence over normal passengers and freight. At Henley station, lighting was much reduced and the edges of the platforms were whitewashed. Train services returned to normal in 1918 but in September 1919 the railway workers at Henley, as elsewhere, came out on strike for increased pay and better working conditions. The strike lasted for about ten days and, as well causing problems for commuters, it meant that milk had to be taken from Henley to London by lorry instead of by train. Later, during the 1920 and '30s, Henley station was probably at its busiest, with a staff of between 24 and 27 who dealt with passengers, loaded and unloaded goods items and unloaded the coal arriving by train. For about thirty years prior to 1920, the GWR itself carried out the collection and delivery of goods in the Henley area and had its own horses and carts for the purpose. However, by 1920 the parcel service was beginning to decline and Toomer & Co. were appointed as delivery agents.

Railway workers took part in the General Strike of 1926, being away from work for 11 days. However, a few trains travelled to and from Henley during this period, being operated by volunteer drivers and firemen. The strike made life difficult for those working in London and resulted in a lack of daily newspapers, but otherwise had little impact on life in Henley.

8

Henley during the 1930s and the Second World War

Increasing Affluence

The 1930s were a period of increasing affluence for those people in employment. However, for much of the decade a substantial number of people in Henley, which in 1931 had a population of just over 7,000, were 'out of work' and relying on the dole. Henley had a large number of shops, most of which were small and family-run: there were several grocers, butchers, bakers, greengrocers and confectioners, together with chemists, dress shops, shoe shops, toy shops, cycle shops, ironmongers and electrical shops. Bell Street was the main shopping street and also housed the surgeries of doctors and dentists, hairdressers and the town's cinema. Some of the older buildings in Bell Street were demolished during the 1930s and replaced by new buildings including a Woolworths store.

In 1933-4, a proposal to replace a Georgian building in Hart Street by a modern cinema in typical 1930s style gave rise to an early campaign to retain the character of the centre of Henley. The proposal, by the Regal (Henley) Company, involved demolishing the Georgian frontage and much of the interior of 18 Hart Street, nearly opposite the *White Hart*. Local opinion on the merits of the proposal was divided, but the plans were passed by the Town Council and by the South Oxfordshire Joint Town Planning Committee. Opposition to the scheme then grew and the opponents were backed by, among others, Lord Hambleden, Lord Camoys, Major Mackenzie, Colonel Leonard Noble and Captain Eric Noble, as well as by the Master of University College, Oxford. Letters opposing the scheme were published in *The Times*. Meanwhile the Henley Cinematograph Company began rebuilding the Picture Palace in Bell Street and, while work was still in progress, the cinema was purchased by the Regal Company and the Hart Street proposal dropped. The new Regal opened in 1937. The Kenton theatre was also renovated for use as a repertory theatre during the 1930s but with limited success in terms of profitability. Another building erected in the mid-1930s, though it appears at first sight to be several centuries old, was Tudor House, near the corner of Duke Street and Friday Street; it was rebuilt from recycled brick and timber, and given its present name. The construction of a new Roman Catholic Church in Vicarage Road was started in about 1936, though it was not consecrated until 1948. It has a stained glass window by Pugin.

Nearly all the large country houses around Henley were still privately occupied during the 1930s, and a lad employed by Budgens, the grocers in Henley, spent almost one whole day each week cycling to the various houses to take orders from the butler or cook for goods to be delivered later.

The attractions of Henley, as advertised in *Salter's Guide to the Thames*, included 'public riverside grounds (hard tennis courts, bowls, putting greens), boating (in the most charming reaches of the Thames), bathing (from well-equipped Corporation Baths

88 *A narrow escape for Henley's heritage – an architect's drawing of the cinema proposed, in 1933, as a replacement for the Georgian building at 18 Hart Street.*

89 Left: *The Regal Cinema which stood in Bell Street, 1937-85.*

90 Right: *Not what it seems – Tudor House, rebuilt in this style and re-named in the 1930s. (Photograph, 2006)*

in the open river), delightful drives and walks (amidst river, woodland and common scenery) and five golf courses within easy reach'. The 'public riverside ground' was at Mill Meadow, which had been acquired by the Town Council in the early 1920s and the ground level raised by about two feet using material dredged from the Regatta course. The Corporation Baths were still by the river at Solomon's Hatch off the Wargrave Road, as they had been in Emily Climenson's time.

During the 1930s, few Henley residents owned cars, and social activities depended largely on the various local churches, clubs and societies. The churches were much involved in providing facilities for the younger generation, one example being the Trinity Hall Lads Brigade, which gave its members access to a wide range of sports, hobbies and excursions. The activities included carpentry, metalwork, boxing and gymnastics.

The disposal of rubbish and waste continued to present problems for the town and there was much criticism of the service provided by a contractor who was paid £720 per year to make a weekly collection by horse-drawn cart. Eventually the Council decided to purchase its own motor vehicle and employ its own drivers and loaders. Some refuse was being disposed of by burning it in a 'Refuse Destructor' and some was buried in various pits around the town, most of which had been excavated in the past as a source of gravel for building and roadworks. Local tips, including one near the end of Lambridge Wood Road, continued to be used until the 1950s.

Another major extension of the town boundary was made in 1932, when parts of the parishes of Badgemore, Rotherfield Greys, Rotherfield Peppard and Harpsden were incorporated into the borough. The newly acquired areas included Swiss Farm and part of Fawley Meadows, land on both sides of the Fair Mile and, to the west of the town centre, Friar Park, Rotherfield Court and Parkside. They also included the area now occupied by housing around Wootton Road and Elizabeth Road, together with an area extending southwards from Peppard Lane to include Rotherfield Road and Drawback Hill and eastwards to the river. The parish of Rotherfield Peppard lost its riverside section and, since then, Henley's boundary has adjoined the parish of Harpsden.

Planning in the 1930s

The lack of significant planning control continued into the 1930s, but by 1931 an Oxfordshire Regional Planning Committee had been formed and this commissioned a report into the needs for, and constraints on, the future development of various areas within the county. The report, one of whose authors was Patrick Abercrombie, who later became an influential town planner, concluded in regard to the Henley District:

> This district requires special consideration on account of its popularity as a boating centre, the importance of its world-renowned Regatta, and the beauty of the river and its surroundings. A carefully considered town-planning scheme is essential. Building should not be allowed to spread in a disorganised fashion but should be confined to predetermined areas. The river frontage and adjoining lands, both above and below the bridge, together with the whole of the regatta course, should be most carefully preserved. The beautiful 'Fair Mile' must not be encroached upon, but with its wide stretches of grass and its stately elms must also be carefully preserved. A limit should be set to the extension of the town in a westerly direction, and in a like manner the eastward extension

91 *Fair Mile undergoing re-surfacing, probably in the 1930s.*

of Caversham should be limited, so that the two towns shall remain completely distinct as they are now, with a wide stretch of open agricultural country between them. The layout of new building sites should be such that the beauty and attractiveness of the town shall be enhanced, and every opportunity taken of getting rid of unworthy buildings.

The planning authorities of the post-war years have generally attempted to adhere to these guidelines despite the great pressures for additional house-building. Although both Henley and Caversham have expanded, their extent has been limited and much of the recommended 'wide stretch of open agricultural country' remains, though it is constantly under threat of piecemeal encroachment. And in Henley itself, it is questionable whether the attractiveness of the town has been enhanced by new building, and whether every opportunity has been taken to get rid of unworthy buildings. The 1931 report also stated:

Suggestions have been made of the construction of a second bridge at Henley and for by-passing the town. It has not up to the present been shown that a new bridge is necessary, there being no congestion of traffic upon or near to the bridge but there is a serious congestion in Bell Street, which is very narrow. Having regard to the beauty of the present bridge, the difficulty of improving the approaches and the danger of destroying the regatta reach by crossing it with an entirely new bridge, and the circuitous nature of any by-pass that could reasonably be constructed to avoid these obstacles, we consider that the project should be indefinitely postponed.

Although congestion is now more serious, the view expressed in this last sentence is still valid.

The Impact of the Second World War

The outbreak of war in September 1939 soon brought major changes to life in Henley, as elsewhere in the country, changes that were recorded in a book by Charles Gray of Hambleden. At the beginning of the war, everyone, including children, was issued with an identity card giving his or her name and address and a specific number. The card had to be shown to any police officer or any member of the armed forces who was on duty and who asked to see it. Early in the war, the Oxford and Bucks regiment was involved in heavy fighting in northern France, though the total of 72 Henley servicemen killed during the war was less than half the total in the First World War. Civilians were recruited into organisations such as the Home Guard, the Air Raid Wardens, the Auxiliary Fire Service, the Red Cross, the Women's Voluntary Service, and the Women's Land Army, all of which had active members in Henley. Stuart Turner Ltd had its own Home Guard platoon, recruited from employees, which had 46 members in 1940.

Food rationing and clothes rationing were introduced, based on coupons which had to be given up, together with the price in cash, whenever rationed items were purchased. Although everyone was issued with a food ration book that contained a year's supply of coupons for items such as meat, bacon, eggs, cheese, butter or margarine, sugar, tea and sweets, there was no guarantee that the food was available. Shopkeepers sometimes had insufficient stock to supply the whole ration to all their customers, even when the ration was as low as, for example, two ounces of butter per person per week. The government organised campaigns to increase food production and to recycle important materials, particularly iron and aluminium. 'Dig for Victory' leaflets were distributed, encouraging householders to cultivate their gardens for vegetables and fruit. Some people also kept chickens as a source of eggs and meat. These measures enabled those who had sufficient time and garden space to augment their rations and alleviate some of the shortages. School children were encouraged to collect rose hips from the surrounding countryside, and these were sent for processing to make the 'rose hip syrup' that was allocated to young children to boost their intake of vitamin C. Kitchen waste was recycled for feeding to pigs and, in Henley, a local farmer was making collections for pig swill as early as 1940.

The shortage of supply applied not only to food and clothing but also to various building materials and items needed for DIY work. There was a huge requirement for metals in the production of munitions and aircraft, and in 1942 the government started to requisition iron railings, unless they were essential for safety or had special architectural significance. Railings were removed from the front gardens of many houses in Henley, and evidence of this removal can still be seen in some of the roads in the town, especially in Queen Street where several front gardens have low brick walls capped with the rounded cement finish left by the railing removers. There was a complete lack of petrol for most people as it was available only to those involved in providing essential services, but buses and taxis continued to run, the taxis sometimes being powered by town gas, carried in bags on the roofs.

As in the First World War, government priorities again caused disruption on the railways, and there were additional measures that caused difficulties for passengers, such as the removal of station name-boards and the almost complete elimination of lighting. On the Thames, there was a resurgence in goods traffic, and the total load carried on the non-tidal river almost doubled between 1939 and 1944, reaching over 600,000 tons.

In order to support the war effort, civilians were encouraged to raise funds, and by January 1941 the town had contributed more than £5,000 specifically for the production of Spitfire aircraft. This project was of local interest, as Spitfire components were produced in workshops in Reading and assembled in an underground factory near Warren Row. The aircraft were then completed and flown for test purposes from a temporary airfield

92   *Queen Street, showing the garden railings removed during the Second World War.*

at Cockpole Green. As well as the underground factory at Warren Row, another, with an entrance on the Wargrave Road, was constructed under the hillside near Park Place. For a number of years it was used by Howden Aircrew Ltd, and some years after the war it became the emergency headquarters of army staff for the South East Region. The site was sold by the Ministry of Defence in 1998 and purchased by a data storage company.

Various measures were taken during the war as precautions against the threat of air raids and the possibility of invasion. Underground shelters were built in various places, including Station Road and the grounds of the National School on Gravel Hill. An air raid siren was installed on the roof of Henley Town Hall, and this could be heard clearly as far away as Hambleden. During the bombing of London in 1940, the sky over White Hill was often lit up at night by the fires more than 30 miles away. Householders had to black out all their windows at night to avoid the possibility of towns being spotted from enemy planes and, for the same reason, there was no street lighting. To confuse a potential invading army, signposts were removed from road junctions, and the names of towns chiselled from some of the local milestones, as can still be seen on the Oxford road between Bix and Nettlebed.

Another impact of the war in Henley was the arrival of evacuees from London, both as individuals and in groups, many of whom were billeted on local families. Christ Church was used as a reception centre where the evacuees met their host families. Henley Grammar School received evacuees from London schools, an arrangement that involved classrooms being used on a shift basis, and Park Place was occupied by North Kensington School. A British Restaurant was opened in Henley to provide basic meals at a minimum price, and this was particularly useful for evacuees and for people working long hours. The WVS arranged for a hand-drawn map to be printed, mainly for the benefit of evacuees, showing the location in the town of various landmarks and important facilities such as air raid shelters and the British Restaurant. Another innovation was the first

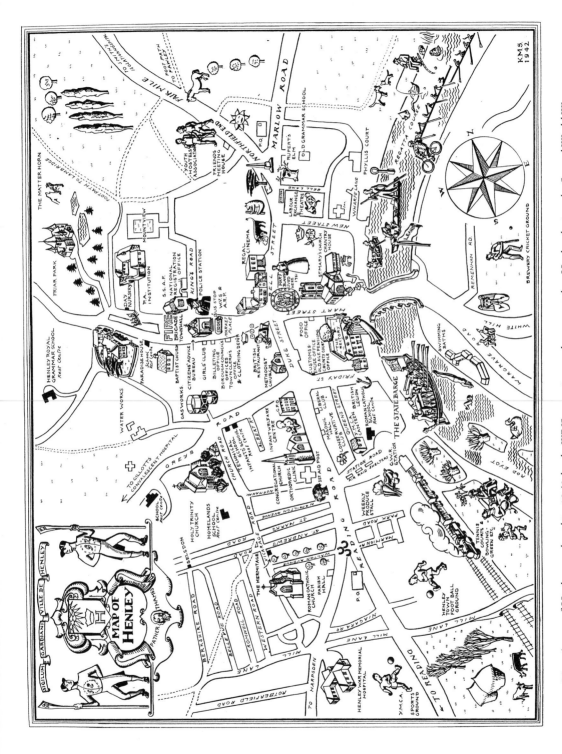

93　　*A map of Henley, produced in 1942 by the WVS, to assist people evacuated to Henley during the Second World War.*

public library in Henley, organised by volunteers, initially intended only for children but, in 1943, made available to adults as well. In 1944, the library was taken over by the Town Council and installed in the basement of the Town Hall.

As well as evacuees from London, many foreign refugees, mostly from Poland, were housed in huts at Kingwood Common and elsewhere in the district, and American and Polish troops were stationed in the woods at Nettlebed. The Americans in particular boosted local trade by making use of the town's pubs and taxis. British forces, too, were stationed in the area while they underwent training, and a number of buildings in the town were used as temporary accommodation, though many of the troops were housed in tents. The Seaforth Highlanders, the Devonshire Regiment and the Surrey Regiment all spent some time in Henley. Large military vehicles added new hazards to the roads, and a bus travelling from Watlington to Reading collided with a tank near Lower Assendon.

By April 1944, the commercial laundry in Henley had so much work from the British and American services that normal customers were discouraged with the slogan 'Is your Bundle Really Necessary?' Also in 1944, the Henley Home Guard Entertainments Committee raised £650 for the Henley Prisoners of War Fund by holding a dance in the Town Hall. In the same year, a new type of threat to the civilians of south-east England appeared – the V1 flying bomb, generally known as the 'doodlebug'. The V1s were targeted at London from northern France and, as a result, a new influx of evacuees arrived in towns to the north and west of London. At the end of July 1944 there were more than 1,000 evacuees in Henley, and by the end of the summer four, but only four, V1s had landed in the surrounding area. However, air raids with conventional aircraft had ceased and the 'blackout' ended in September. The *Henley Standard* reported that there was 'quite an appreciable crowd' in the Market Place, and there were subdued cheers when the street lights came on.

The Beginning of Recovery

Following the end of the war in Europe, the Henley VE Day parade on 13 May 1945 was filmed by Mr Machins, a local vet who was also an amateur photographer and had been able to acquire some colour cine film, probably from a contact in the American services. The film, of which the original is now in the Imperial War Museum, shows a large number of people in various organisations taking part in the parade through Henley but a relatively small number of people watching. Later in the day, crowds assembled in the Market Place to take part in dancing and a torchlight procession to the Makins recreation ground where an effigy of Hitler was burnt.

Life began to return to normal after the end of the war but shortages continued and, in fact, bread was rationed for the first time in July 1946. Shortages were aggravated by the severe winter of 1946-7, when electricity cuts were common, and the winter was followed by flooding sufficiently severe for people living in Mill Lane to be rescued by Sherman tanks. There was renewed emphasis on house-building and in Henley, as in other towns, an estate of cheap prefabricated bungalows was erected. This was at The Close, off Greys Road, and although the 'prefabs' were meant to be only a short-term solution to the housing shortage, the estate at The Close remained until 1982-5, when it was steadily replaced by brick-built houses, flats and bungalows.

In 1948, the Olympic rowing events were, as in 1908, held at Henley, again separately from the Regatta.

9

The 1950s Onwards

Buildings and Open Spaces

The post-war expansion of housing continued into the 1950s and beyond. The Gainsborough estate of council housing was begun in 1946 and finished in the early 1950s. Houses were built in Manor Road during the years 1957-9 and in Elizabeth Road at about the same time. Ancastle Green, Milton Close, Damer Gardens and Baronsmead were all developed during the 1960s. Milton Close was built on the site of Paradise House, once the home of William Brakspear but demolished in the 1950s. The houses in Blandy Road, Makins Road, Wootton Road and the upper part of St Andrews Road were built around 1963-4, those in Deanfield Road and Valley Road in 1968-70 and those in the Luker Avenue/ Crisp Road area in the early 1970s. Many of the new houses built during the 1960s and early '70s were occupied by people moving into the town from elsewhere and, from the mid-1970s, it became clear that the main need for further housing in Henley was for low-cost homes for local people, with some available for renting. Houses and flats at Mount View, at the Close replacing the prefabs, and at Noble Road were built to meet this need.

Throughout the post-war period and up to the present time, a number of other houses, usually detached, have been built on plots of land that had previously been parts of the gardens of larger pre-war houses. There have been relatively few major changes in the buildings in the shopping area but the range of goods sold in the smaller shops has changed considerably, reflecting the building of a Waitrose supermarket in the mid-1960s, a new Boots store in the 1970s and a Tesco superstore on the edge of the town in 1995. Additional accommodation for light industry was made available at Newtown Road from about 1965 onwards, providing an opportunity for several local businesses to relocate to more suitable premises.

Henley's population increased during the post-war period from about 8,000 in 1951 to more than 11,000 in 1971 but later declined slightly, despite additional house-building, to 10,700 in 2001. The public library was run by Oxfordshire County Council from 1965 onwards and a new building to house it, in Ravenscroft Road, was opened in 1981.

Most of the houses and offices built in Henley since the First World War have been of standard types and, in 1965, were criticised by the local architect Lionel Brett (later Lord Esher) in his book, *Landscape in Distress*, as being of too low density and of poor design. However, a few more recent individual buildings do have distinctive characteristics, for example the Regatta Headquarters, the River & Rowing Museum and Perpetual House. The Regatta headquarters, on the Berkshire side of Henley Bridge, was completed in 1986, replacing an old pub, the *Carpenters Arms*, and several boat-sheds. The building was designed by Terry Farrell and gained several design awards. About two years later, the

94 *The Regatta Headquarters, newly built in 1986.*

River & Rowing Museum, designed by David Chipperfield, was opened and won the Royal Fine Art Commission's 'Building of the Year' award. The walls of the ground floor are mainly glass, while those of the upper floor are covered in oak cladding. Inside the museum there are three main sections, one illustrating various features of the River Thames and its role in human history, another the development of Henley with artefacts and memorabilia from the past, and the third the historical development of rowing. Perpetual House, an office building in Station Road, was constructed in 1994 for the Perpetual Unit Trust company, founded and managed by Martyn (now Sir Martyn) Arbib, whose home was near Henley. However, following the construction of new premises for what is now Invesco Perpetual Ltd, off Reading Road, Perpetual House is likely to be converted to apartments.

Since the early 1990s, almost all new housing in Henley has been built on so-called 'brown-field' sites which, by government definition, have included the gardens of older houses, as well as the actual sites of previous buildings. This policy has therefore resulted in a loss of spaciousness and of some trees in the town. Developments on brown-field sites have included three blocks of apartments: on the corner of Reading Road and Hamilton Avenue, replacing a pub (2005); on the corner of Reading Road and Norman Avenue, replacing the premises of Thames Carpets (2006), and on the corner of Greys Road and Green Lane, replacing a single detached house (2006).

During the 1950s and '60s the Market Place continued to be an open space that was available for car parking but in 1974, after the provision of other car parks in the town, the centre of the Market Place was converted into a paved precinct surrounded by a low wall and pleached lime trees. In 1996 there was a highly controversial proposal to pedestrianise the Market Place completely but, after a trial period, a compromise involving partial pedestrianisation was adopted in 2001. York stone paving was laid,

95 *The Market Place showing its use as a car park during the 1950s.*

96
The Market Place/ Falaise Square as it was between 1974 and 1999.

new trees were planted, the north side was closed to traffic, and one-way traffic on the south side was restricted to 20 m.p.h.

The Town Council has continued to add to the areas available for public access. Marsh Meadows, next to the smaller Mill Meadow, were purchased in 1968 and this greatly extended the area open to the public. A number of trees were planted and a small section has been designated a wildlife area. Another substantial open space that was acquired in the early 1990s is Gillott's Corner Field, which provides a roughly rectangular walk of about one mile and also includes a footpath that leads to the Harpsden Valley. Two thousand trees and shrubs were planted in and around the field by local volunteers in the year 2000.

Henley and its buildings have featured in the work of two well-known individuals, both of whom lived within about five miles of Henley for much of the post-war period: the artist John Piper, and the novelist, scriptwriter and barrister, John (now Sir John) Mortimer.

97   *The Market Place/ Falaise Square as it has been since 2001.*

Changes in Local Government

Until 1974, Henley had the status of a borough. From the 1500s until 1974, its town councillors had much more influence over the management of the town than they had before or have had since. For most of that period, the Town Council was responsible for all local services, though after about 1900 matters concerned with health, planning, education and policing were dealt with by the County Council. The Thames Valley Police Force was formed in 1968, bringing together the forces of Berkshire, Buckinghamshire and Oxfordshire, together with those of the city of Oxford and Reading Borough. In 1974, when the country's local government was re-organised, all the urban and rural districts councils in Oxfordshire were replaced by five district councils, one of which, South Oxfordshire District Council, replaced the councils of Henley Borough, Henley Rural District, Wallingford Borough, Wallingford Rural District, Thame Urban District and Bullingdon Rural District. After this, the responsibilities of Henley Town Council were similar in scope to those of the smaller parish councils, though Henley did retain the position of mayor, who was (and still is) elected each year from a total of 16 councillors. The Council also continued to own and manage various properties in the town and nearby. Since 1974, the County Council has had responsibility for general strategy and for education and highways, while the District Council has had responsibility for local planning, refuse collection and leisure activities.

With the support of the Town Council, Henley twinned, in 1973, with the French town of Falaise in Normandy which was the birthplace of William the Conqueror. In 1979, Henley twinned with the German town of Leichlingen, a centre for fruit and flower growing in the Rhineland area. And, since 1981, Henley has had a friendship link with Borama in Somalia.

Post-war Planning

Virtually no housing had been built anywhere in the country during the Second World War, and when the war ended there was a resurgence in the demand for houses. However, mainly in order to curtail the type of ribbon development that had occurred along many main roads during the 1930s, the Town and Country Planning Act was introduced in 1947. This made almost all building development subject to planning permission and stipulated that the authorisation of planning permission should be transferred from the urban and rural district councils to county councils. Building developments in and around Henley were therefore controlled by Oxfordshire County Council until the next major reorganisation of local government in 1974. The County Council started work on the First Structure Plan for Oxfordshire and, in 1966, produced an 'Informal Town Map' for Henley. This suggested various locations for new housing that included Valley Road and the area near Luker Avenue. It also suggested a new industrial site between the Reading Road and the railway, additional car parks to the north and south of Hart Street, and the possibility of a partial inner ring road. However, the Map was never formally adopted and the suggestions for the additional car parks and inner ring road were not pursued.

A government report, in 1970, from the Joint Planning Team for the South-East Planning Region of England stated:

> Henley-on-Thames is the largest settlement in the predominantly rural area of high landscape value, including part of the Thames Valley and Chilterns. The Structure Plan for the area should suggest positive measures to combine conservation and enhancement of the natural environment with the provision of additional opportunities for recreation. Provision for only very limited population growth is envisaged.

In 1974, responsibility for planning was transferred from the county councils to the newly-formed district councils, and so for Henley to the South Oxfordshire District Council. Soon afterwards, this Council approved a policy statement intended to control the amount of office development in the town, in order to minimise changes in the character of the town centre and to restrain growth in traffic. In 1979, it produced a Local Plan for Henley, taking into account the recommendations of the County Structure Plan that had been issued by the County Council. The Plan set out a number of objectives of which two were: 'to conserve, protect and enhance the special architectural and historic character of the town centre', and 'to protect and preserve the outstanding rural surroundings and approaches into Henley and contain future development within the existing well-defined limits of the town'. No further large-scale expansion was envisaged and the Plan proposed that all new housing should be designed for the needs of local people.

Since 1979, the planning policy has largely conformed to these objectives and restricted the further extension of housing into green-field sites. A serious threat to the policy occurred in 1985-6 when an application was made to extend the built-up area of

Henley beyond the town boundary by building 200 dwellings on Gillott's Corner Field. However, after strong objections to this proposal, the application was finally rejected. The South Oxfordshire Local Plan, 2011, adopted in 2006, proposes a continuation of this general strategy and states that 'There will be no significant housing growth in Henley'. The only location in the town envisaged as suitable for an appreciable number of houses was considered to be part of the Townlands Hospital site.

The Conservation of Historic Henley

Since 1960, and especially since 1980, the emphasis given to the conservation of historic buildings has slowly but steadily increased. One building in Henley whose retention required a major effort from local residents early in this period was the *Catherine Wheel Hotel*, which has existed since at least 1541. It was threatened with demolition in 1961 as part of a redevelopment scheme to erect shops and maisonettes and, although the plan was rejected by Oxfordshire County Council, there was an appeal against the decision. The threat prompted the formation of a local civic society, the Henley Society, which then acted as a focus for the campaign against the proposal, a campaign supported by national organisations such as the CPRE, the Georgian Group and the Council for British Archaeology. Eventually the appeal was refused and the *Catherine Wheel* was retained as a pub and restaurant.

Another building that was retained largely due to the efforts of local residents was the Kenton Theatre, thought to be the fourth oldest working theatre in England. The lease of the Kenton had been taken over by two local residents in 1951, and a new arch over the front of the stage was designed and painted by John Piper, who lived a few miles from the town. There were some successful amateur productions during the next few years, but in 1962 the building was declared unsafe. It was threatened with demolition in 1965, but a group of local residents campaigned to save it and organised a complete renovation. The theatre is now run by the Kenton Theatre Management Society, which organises a programme that includes productions by the Henley Amateur Operatic and Dramatic Society, productions by visiting companies and also films. The 200th anniversary of the opening was celebrated in 2005 with a revival of the original production, *The School of Reform* by Thomas Morton.

During the late 1980s, a building of concern to many residents was the Regal cinema that dated from 1937. A major expansion of the Waitrose supermarket was planned in a scheme that involved demolishing the Regal, and this aspect of the proposal angered many protesters, including George Harrison of the Beatles. Nevertheless, the scheme went ahead and the old Regal was demolished, but it was replaced by a new three-screen Regal cinema in the redevelopment which opened in 1997.

More recently, the so-called 'Barn' behind the former *Kings Arms*, which was built in about 1600, has been conserved, largely thanks to the Town Council. Almost certainly it was built not as a barn but as a stable to the *Kings Arms*, with accommodation for travellers over the stabling. When horse traffic declined after 1840, the building was used for a time as stabling for the brewery horses and then for storage, and so was not significantly altered. It was restored during 2000-1, with as many as possible of the original features, including wattle and daub panelling, being retained. The Barn is currently owned by the Town Council and is used as a tourist information office on the ground floor, and as a community hall on the first floor.

The Chantry House, having deteriorated since its renovation in the 1920s, was restored to a high standard in 2003-4 with the help of a grant from the Heritage Lottery Fund, and during the restoration several items of interest including a Latin book dated 1624 were found under the floorboards.

When Brakspears plc ceased their brewing operation in 2002, to become a property company owning about 100 pubs, the site of the brewery was sold for redevelopment. As a condition of planning consent, the frontages of the existing buildings on to New Street and Thameside had to be retained; one of the major buildings facing New Street has been converted into a hotel and bistro, and another into offices.

The Town Hall, built in 1901, has been well maintained and still impresses some visitors. A columnist in *The Times* wrote in 2004, 'Town Hall: do these words sink the heart? Go to a place like Henley-on-Thames and you envy the unchanging almost smug air of civic pride that its charming Town Hall bestows.' Inside the Town Hall, the name of every mayor from 1305 to the present time is engraved on wooden plaques. There are also paintings of Henley by John Piper and, in the Mayor's Parlour, a collection of watercolours by Lucy Cooper. These show various views of Henley as it was in about 1900. In the main hall, there are full-length portraits of George I and of Thomas Parker, who was Earl of Macclesfield and the first High Steward of the town. The portrait of George I was painted by Sir Godfrey Kneller and presented to the Corporation by his widow, who was the daughter of Dr Cawley, a rector of Henley. Among other items is the town seal that was in use from 1305 to 1567 and, again, from 1664 to 1780. On the external wall of the Town Hall, facing the Market Place, are memorials to the servicemen killed in the two world wars.

In 1970, the obelisk, that was originally sited at the crossroads at the centre of the town and was subsequently moved to Northfield End to make way for the fountain, was found to be in the way of a road-widening and roundabout scheme and was moved again, this time to a rather incongruous position in Mill Meadows.

Following the introduction of the Civic Amenities Act of 1967, two Conservation Areas were designated in Henley by the County Council. One covered most of the central area of the town, with extensions along the riverside, around Northfield End, along part of the Fair Mile and up Gravel Hill to the Middle Lodge of Friar Park. The second was centred on Greys Hill and Church Street, and included part of Norman Avenue. A few years later, a third Conservation Area taking in the Edwardian housing in St Mark's and St Andrew's Roads was designated, and then in 2005 a fourth, taking in the terraced housing in the Park Road/ Marmion Road area. Conservation Areas were, and are, selected on the basis of their having sufficient architectural or historic interest to justify preservation and enhancement of their character. They are given additional protection under the Planning Acts so that any changes are subject to more rigorous criteria. Also, all trees with a trunk diameter of more than three inches are protected.

Historic buildings, whether or not they are in a Conservation Area, can also be protected by being 'Listed' individually. This designation indicates that they are of 'special architectural or historic interest'. In the Henley Conservation Area there are 378 listed buildings, of which one, the Chantry House, is grade I and 12 are grade II*. These

98 *A map (of 1927) showing Henley's Conservation Areas, as designated before 2007.*

include St Mary's Church, the Town Hall, the former *Old White Hart* and the former *Bell Hotel*. When any change is proposed to a listed building that affects its architectural character, special Listed Building Consent is required from the planning authority.

The wide verges of the Fair Mile, which have been an important feature of Henley for centuries, have been conserved as open space. Most of the elm trees planted in 1752 were still standing in 1935, when the Fair Mile was described by the author and journalist Cecil Roberts as being 'unsurpassed by any public road in the kingdom', but by 1953 the majority of the elms had died or were in poor condition. The Town Council then decided to replace them by an avenue of Turkey oaks, planted to commemorate the Coronation of Queen Elizabeth II. And, in 1977, an avenue of lime trees was planted inside the oak avenue to commemorate the Queen's Silver Jubilee.

Swan Upping, a practice dating from Elizabethan times, still takes place on the Thames each year. Six traditional rowing skiffs, two belonging to the Crown, two to the Dyers' Company and two to the Vintners' Company, are partly towed and partly rowed from Sunbury to Abingdon during the third week of July. They start on the Monday and finish on the Friday, normally arriving in Henley at about 1.30 p.m. on the Wednesday. During the journey, all the swans encountered are checked and counted, and new cygnets with parents belonging to one of the two companies are marked to indicate their ownership; all unmarked swans automatically become the property of the Crown.

The Health Service

The measures introduced by the National Health Service Act of 1948 brought major changes in health care. Everyone was eligible to register with a GP, and consultations and treatment incurred no direct payment. There were six full-time GPs in Henley in 1950, a number that had increased to 12 by 2006. As a result of the National Health Act, both Townlands Hospital and the War Memorial Hospital were transferred to the National Health Service, which took on responsibility for staff salaries. Townlands Hospital was slowly improved and expanded, but specialist facilities and treatment were increasingly based at Reading. By the late 1970s, the NHS was giving consideration to closing the War Memorial Hospital and, despite strong objections based largely on the grounds that it had been paid for by local subscriptions and that it still provided a useful 'cottage hospital' service, it was finally closed in 1985. The building subsequently became the centre of a private development of 'retirement' flats and bungalows. Townlands Hospital continued to provide long-stay and convalescent facilities for patients, some of whom had been treated at larger hospitals in Reading or Oxford, and it also housed a number of units for out-patient clinics and for minor injuries. During 2005-7, Townlands Hospital itself has been under consideration for further change or possible closure.

From 1952 to 1988, the Smith Hospital was a child psychiatric hospital, but the buildings were sold in 1990 and the site redeveloped for offices, re-named the Smith Centre.

Developments in Education

As a result of the Education Act of 1944, implemented in 1946, all pupils moved at the age of 11 or 12 to a secondary school, either a secondary modern school or, for those who passed the 11-plus exam, a grammar school. The minimum leaving age was raised to 15 and it was expected that pupils at the grammar schools would stay until at least 16. All fees for secondary education were abolished. In Henley, children (other than those attending private schools) attended the Infant School in Greys Road (on the site of the present Goodall Close) from age five to seven. They then proceeded to the Primary School in Greys Hill (with buildings on both sides of the road) until aged 11 or 12. The children then went either to the Secondary Modern School (the renamed National School) in Gravel Hill or to the Grammar School (by then in the house, Rotherfield Court), depending on the results of the 11-plus exam. A few years later, a Girls Technical School was opened at Gillotts House and this provided both commercial and nursing courses, with boarding facilities available for those from surrounding villages. In 1960, this school amalgamated with the Secondary Modern School and, during the next two years, all the pupils moved to the Gillotts School site. Boarding facilities continued there until 1964.

In 1976, the lower forms of the Grammar School were incorporated into what then became Gillotts Comprehensive School, while the 6th form continued at the Grammar School, which became King James College, the first sixth form college in Oxfordshire. Eleven years later King James College merged with the Technical College to form the Henley College.

The Technical Institute had been transferred to Oxfordshire County Council in 1948 and, in 1953, after it had been re-named the Technical College, it moved to premises at 11 Reading Road previously occupied by the Liberal Club. A full-time principal was appointed for the first time, and in 1961-2 the Technical College took over the buildings at Gravel Hill that had been vacated when the Secondary Modern had moved to Gillotts School. It then became the South Oxfordshire Technical College. Over the next 25 years it grew considerably and, in 1987, was combined with King James College to create the first tertiary college in Oxfordshire, providing academic courses to A level, plus a range of vocational training courses and also part-time adult education.

Traffic problems

In recent years, Henley, as elsewhere in the country, has encountered serious traffic congestion, with the A4130 from west London and Slough to Oxford crossing the A4155 from Reading to Marlow and High Wycombe, and with many daily commuters either leaving the town or coming into it. There have been several campaigns for a new bridge across the Thames at Sonning (or some other point between Reading and Marlow) but these have been opposed on the grounds that a new bridge would inevitably increase the pressure for major housing developments on the Oxfordshire side, with a serious impact on attractive Chiltern countryside, and that the additional traffic capacity provided by a new bridge would almost certainly soon be saturated by an increase in traffic.

In Henley itself attempts have been made to minimise the impact of traffic in the town centre by schemes such as the introduction of traffic lights (the first set in 1932), the introduction of one-way streets and the partial pedestrianisation of the Market Place. Some of the roads entering the town have been somewhat widened or straightened, but traffic on the A 4155 still crosses the narrow Conway's Bridge, built by Humphrey Gainsborough (see p.104).

Changes on the River and Railway

The transport of goods by barge on the river continued to be important during the immediate post-war years, but the amount declined steadily after 1950, and was negligible after the early 1960s. However, the decline was counter-balanced by a steady increase in recreational boating, mainly in hired boats. The Henley stretch of the river has been particularly popular, and during the period 1973-97 more boats passed through Marsh Lock than through any of the others, though Boulters Lock at Maidenhead was a close second. Cruising on the river reached its peak of popularity in the 1970s and early 1980s, and since then the number of boats has declined to some extent. Arrangements for the administration of the river have continued to change. The Thames Conservancy became a division of the new Thames Water Authority in 1974, and this was subsequently subsumed into the National Rivers Authority and, since 1993, the Environment Agency.

The railways were nationalised in 1948, a time when road transport was becoming increasingly dominant and the use of the Henley branch, except by commuters, was declining. For several years there were few major changes, and gas lights were present at Henley station until 1963. Diesel railcars were introduced to the branch line in 1958 but steam trains continued to be used on some of the through trains to London until 1963. At about that time, the sidings were removed and the engine shed and goods shed demolished. The branch line was reduced from double to single track in the early 1970s and the width of the bridge over the Thames near Shiplake was halved. In 1975 the station, dating from 1904, was largely demolished and replaced by a modern building that incorporated shops and commercial offices as well a railway booking office. Then, in 1986, a new but small station was built about 70 yards down the track from the original station and the number of platforms reduced from two to one. A new commercial office building was constructed, and the site of the old goods yard was converted into a car park. In 2007, as in 1900, there were two through trains each morning to Paddington, taking about 50 minutes, and three in the return direction in the evening to Henley.

The Regatta

The Regatta regained its popularity after the Second World War. Competitors at the Regatta have come in increasing numbers from all over the world and, for many of the 18 events, it has become necessary to hold qualifying races during the previous week. Even so, in recent years there have often been about 100 races per day during the earlier days of the Regatta, with starts at five-minute intervals. And, as each race takes about seven minutes, this has resulted in two races being on the course at the same time, each followed by a launch with an umpire on board. Since 1986, when it was extended to five days, the Regatta has started on the Wednesday preceding the first Saturday in July, and finished on the following Sunday evening. The number of 'spectators', many of them not interested in the rowing, reached a peak in the late 1980s, boosted by a surge in the amount of corporate entertaining. It was estimated in 1988 that the official caterers stocked up with 50,000 bottles of Pimms, 14,000 pints of bitter, 6,000 bottles of champagne, 3,000 lb of strawberries and over 1,000 lb of lobster. In 2005 the cost of staging the Regatta amounted to £1.76 million but the income exceeded this figure by about £485,000. The year 2005 was also notable as being the first year in which the Henley Rowing Club won an open event in the Regatta, the Thames Cup.

10

A Who's Who of Street Names

Some of the street names in Henley reflect their destination (e.g. Marlow Road and Harpsden Road), some reflect their particular location (e.g. Western Road and Mount View) and some are derived from the names of inns (e.g. Hart Street and Bell Street), but many commemorate individuals who have had a connection with the town. In some instances the individuals have had a national importance, in others they are of just local significance, but the choice of them provides insights into the history of the town.

Abrahams Road
The houses in Abrahams Road were built, in the 1970s, on land that was previously part of the Abrahams allotments, and it is thought a Mr Abrahams was the owner of the area when it was just a field.

Albert Road
Named after Prince Albert (1819-61), the husband of Queen Victoria, who was the first royal patron of Henley Regatta. His popularity was also enhanced by his initiative in promoting the Great Exhibition held in Hyde Park in 1851.

Blandy Road
Blandy Road commemorates Francis and Mary Blandy, the former a well-respected Town Clerk of Henley whose death by poisoning in 1751 still poses unanswered questions. Having been widowed, Francis Blandy continued to live with his daughter Mary, who acted as hostess for his dinner parties and other social activities. However, both Mary and her father became increasingly keen for her to be married, and he is thought to have rather exaggerated his daughter's likely inheritance in an attempt to attract a prospective husband with a desirable social background. About £10,000 is the sum usually mentioned. This tactic had the unfortunate consequence of attracting a Captain Cranston who, though an officer in a Scottish regiment, had the reputation of being a fortune seeker and already married, with a wife in Scotland. Despite warnings from her father, Mary welcomed Cranston's attention and hoped to marry him. Having returned to Scotland, Cranston sent Mary a package which included some white powder, probably arsenic, that she was told to mix with her father's food and drink. Soon after the package arrived, Francis Blandy became ill, as did two female servants who had eaten some food that he had left. Poisoning was suspected but Francis Blandy was reluctant to accept that Mary might have been responsible. Although his suspicions became stronger, he is said to have forgiven his daughter shortly before he died, placing the blame entirely on Cranston. Rumours that he had been poisoned were circulating in the town and, when he died, Mary was the main suspect. She

99   *Mary Blandy in leg irons in Oxford Gaol but taking tea with a visiting friend.*

decided to leave Henley and offered a manservant £500 to accompany her, but he refused. Later, when she attempted to leave the house by herself, she was surrounded by townspeople near the bridge and arrested by a constable 'for her own safety'. An inquest held into the death of Francis Blandy confirmed that he had been poisoned and, as a result, Mary was accused of murder and imprisoned in Oxford Gaol. At her trial, she maintained that Cranston had told her that the white powder would make her father more amenable, and more likely to agree to their marriage. However, this did not convince the jury and she was convicted and executed by hanging, aged 32, in April 1752. Despite her conviction, she was buried, at 1a.m., in Henley church alongside the bodies of her parents, an unusual burying place for someone condemned as a murderess. Even at that time, in the middle of the night, a large number of people attended the funeral, suggesting perhaps that sympathies had changed. Cranston had fled to France and, lacking cash, lodged in a monastery where, a little later, he became ill and died, possibly having taken poison himself. J.S. Burn wrote more than 100 years later that the Blandy affair had caused 'a most unprecedented sensation throughout the nation', and the controversy over whether Mary Blandy had criminal intent or was just naïve has never been resolved.

The Blandy family lived at a house with a large bay window, where Blandy House in Hart Street now stands. The house was rebuilt in about 1850 for private occupation but is now occupied by dental surgeries.

Chalcraft Close
Named after John Chalcraft (1897-1985) who worked at Brakspears Brewery for 70 years until 1974, latterly as managing director. He was the Mayor of Henley in 1936-8 and also a member of Oxfordshire County Council. He was a keen supporter of Henley Golf Club.

Clarence Road
The houses in Clarence Road, and those in York Road, were built around 1900, so it is likely that the road was named after the Duke of Clarence (1866-92), who was the eldest son of the Prince of Wales (who became Edward VII) and a grandson of Queen Victoria. The Duke died at the age of 26, leaving the Duke of York, the future King George V, as heir to the throne.

Clements Road

Charles Clements was born in West Street in 1845 and became an increasingly successful building contractor. At one time he employed more than 100 men. He was the main contractor for the house at Friar Park House, and he also built most of the houses in Norman Avenue as well as other houses in the town. He was Mayor of Henley on several occasions: in 1885, 1892 and from 1901 to 1903. When the Council decided to build a new Town Hall, he gained the contract to demolish the old one and then rebuilt it as a private house for himself at Crazies Hill. Clements became a leading member of the temperance movement in the town and was involved in lobbying Parliament to restrict drinking hours. He also criticised the large number of drinking establishments in Henley (62 licensed premises for a population of just over 5,000) as the cause of a large amount of drunkenness. In the election for the newly formed Oxfordshire County Council in 1888, he stood, unsuccessfully, as a Henley candidate against Archibald Brakspear who represented the brewing and innkeeping interests in the town. When a fire broke out at Clements' workshops behind his house in Market Place, it was suspected to have been started by opponents of his temperance campaign, though the actual source of the fire was never identified.

Cooper Road

Five members of the Cooper family became, in succession, Town Clerks of Henley. The road is probably named after the last, John Frederick Cooper (1855-1928), who was educated at Marlborough College, became a solicitor, and was Town Clerk from 1896 to 1914. He was also Secretary to the Regatta for 37 years and a founder member of Henley Golf Club. One of his sisters was Lucy Cooper (1853-1929), whose watercolour paintings of Henley in the years around 1900 are in the Mayor's Parlour at the Town Hall.

Crisp Road

Frank Crisp (1843-1919) was a successful and wealthy solicitor in the City of London, a partner in the firm of Ashurst, Morris & Crisp that specialised in company law. While living in London, his daily routine, according to Judy Slinn, was to arrive at his office at 9.45, have only a bar of chocolate for lunch, take tea and toast at 4 p.m. and dinner at 6.45, return to his office at 8 p.m. and work till 10 p.m., with one of his clerks staying on to take dictation. However, he also found time to be a Fellow of the Royal Microscopical Society, and to be a collector of microscopes and 'all that is microscopically interesting'. In about 1890 he purchased the house and land at Friar Park and

100 *Sir Frank Crisp, a successful London lawyer who commissioned the building of Friar Park and lived there from 1895 to 1919.*

had the present house (see p. 117) built to his specifications. He moved there with his wife and children in 1895, and by 1900 had spent about £150,000 on the house and grounds. His daily routine changed to weekly commuting: he left Henley by train on Monday morning, was met at Paddington station by a horse-drawn brougham and was driven to the city, dictating to a clerk during the journey. He left the office on Friday afternoon and was driven to Paddington, again accompanied by a clerk taking dictation. Lucrative contracts continued to come his way and in 1907 he drew up the agreements covering the cutting of the largest diamond in the world, the Cullinan diamond of just over 3000 carats. Frank Crisp was also an adviser to the Liberal Party and was knighted in 1907 and created a baronet in 1913. After moving to Henley, he made substantial donations to the town and organisations within it. For example, in January 1907 he provided an entertainment in the Town Hall for all 1,300 children of the town, split between two successive Saturdays.

Cromwell Road

This road was presumably named after Oliver Cromwell, who was a leader of the Parliamentarians in the Civil War. He established the Protectorate as a replacement for the Monarchy, and this lasted from 1653 to 1657. During the Civil War, the Parliamentarians had the local support of Sir Bulstrode Whitelock of Fawley Court and General Bartholomew Hall.

Damer Gardens

The Hon. Mrs Anne Damer (1749-1828) was the daughter of General Conway of Park Place and also a cousin of Horace Walpole. Her husband, John Damer, committed suicide after accumulating large debts through gambling and horse racing, and she was left with little financial support. She then made her living from sculpture, for which she had already shown some aptitude, and became sufficiently skilful to gain commissions for a statue of George III and a bust of Nelson. In Henley, she contributed to the town's heritage by carving the two heads, of Thamesis and Isis, on the keystones of Henley Bridge, the head of Isis being based on a daughter of Sambrook Freeman of Fawley Court. She also exhibited 30 works at the Royal Academy between 1784 and 1818. In later life, Mrs Damer inherited Strawberry Hill, a well-known house in Twickenham, from Horace Walpole.

Gainsborough Road

Humphrey Gainsborough's father was a Suffolk trader who at various times was a clothier, an innkeeper and a postmaster. The painter Thomas Gainsborough was Humphrey's younger brother. Humphrey studied to become a nonconformist minister, following the example set by an uncle, and was appointed as minister of the Independent Chapel in Henley in 1749, with a stipend of £60 per year. Alongside his commitment to his religion, he had a continuing interest and skill in engineering which brought him to the attention of the local landowners. Encouraged by Sambrooke Freeman of Fawley Court, he designed several items of industrial and agricultural equipment and won at least two competition prizes, for designs for a tide-mill and a drill plough. He also produced the first fire-proof safe – a cast-iron box with a lid of ⅜ inch thickness and a sophisticated lock. Thomas Hall of Harpsden Court, who supported Gainsborough in his role at the Independent Chapel, is also thought to have provided him with workshop accommodation.

When General Conway of Park Place decided in 1763 to improve the Henley to Wargrave road by building a bridge over the so-called 'Happy Valley', he contracted Gainsborough to supervise the structural engineering. The high quality of the work is shown by the fact that traffic on the busy Henley-Wargrave road still crosses his bridge. In 1768 Gainsborough was involved in another project instigated by General Conway. This was to reduce the slope of White Hill by removing earth from the top of the hill and using it to form a ramp at the bottom. Gainsborough's system of ropes and pulleys enabled empty carts to be pulled up the slope by the weight of carts taking earth down the slope, greatly reducing the manpower needed. The scale of this operation is now largely hidden by trees and bushes but the height of the ramp can be seen clearly from Matson Drive. Once completed, the project made it much easier for carriages and wagons with heavy loads to climb the hill, whereas previously there were

101 *Humphrey Gainsborough (1716-73), Minister at the Independent Chapel and an inventor of engineering equipment.*

102 *White Hill, still white from its chalk surface.*

two unwelcome options. One was to hire extra horses from the inn at the bottom of the hill, a profitable enterprise for the innkeeper, and the other was to make a lengthy diversion via Remenham Lane and Aston.

A few years later, Gainsborough was asked to oversee the construction of eight locks on the Thames, to replace the old flash locks, between Maidenhead and Sonning. These were completed in 1772-3 and Gainsborough was then appointed as collector of the lock tolls from Hambleden to Sonning. However, he died suddenly one day, aged 57, on his way home from collecting the tolls. Humphrey Gainsborough's achievements appear to have been under-rated by history, perhaps because he had no family successors and his inventions were simply taken over and adapted by later engineers. His life was summarised in an article in the *Gentleman's Magazine* in 1788:

> Mr Gainsborough possessed as strong a genius for mechanics as his brother, the artist, had for painting … Few men were ever more respected than this worthy divine, he was as eminent for humanity, simplicity and integrity as he was for genius.

Goodall Close
Goodall Close was named after Miss Queenie Goodall, who started teaching at the Henley National Infants School in 1926 and whose family ran an ironmongery shop in the town. After a few years she moved to the newly built Infants School in Greys Road, and was headmistress there from 1936 to 1966. The buildings became part of the South Oxfordshire Technical College but were sold in 1990 and Goodall Close was built on the site in about 2000.

Gravett Close
William Gravett, in his will of 1664, bequeathed sufficient funds to employ a schoolmaster for the Grammar School and to provide a house for him. He also left, or possibly donated before his death, three dwellings in Friday Street whose rents were to be for the benefit of the Corporation of Henley. An amount of £15 was intended for poor relief, £2 for maintaining the bridge and a further amount for curbing the turbulent element of the town's population.

Hamilton Avenue
William and Thomas Hamilton were brothers who built a large number of late Victorian and Edwardian terraced houses in Henley, including many of those in Reading Road, Harpsden Road and Kings Road. Albert Road was built in the late 1880s by William Hamilton, who intended to continue the road to connect with Norman Avenue, but this plan was thwarted by Charles Clements who was building larger houses in Norman Avenue. The Hamiltons had visited North America and their visit is thought to account for the occurrence of Boston Road, Niagara Road and Quebec Road, all off the Reading Road. Thomas Hamilton was also responsible for the houses in the Park Road/ Marmion Road area. William Hamilton was Mayor of Henley in 1916.

Harcourt Close
In 1199, the manor of Bensington, together with the town and manor of Henley, was granted by King John to Robert de Harcourt, the head of a Norman family.

103   *Building workers employed by Thomas Hamilton, c.1910.*

Haywards Close
This name is derived from William Hayward, the architect who designed the present bridge over the Thames. The bridge was completed in 1786 but Hayward died, aged 41, soon after work on the bridge had started. He was buried in St Mary's Church and there is a tablet to his memory on the interior of the wall supporting the tower.

Hobbs End
The houses in Hobbs End are built on the site of the demolished *A E Hobbs* pub that was sold to developers in the 1990s. Mr A.E. Hobbs was born in 1871 and for many years was an architect employed by Brakspears. In this role he was responsible for the design of several pubs in the area. From 1895, he was for many years a member of Henley Town Council. He was also well known as a fisherman and, during the 55-year period between 1890 and 1945, caught 878 trout over 3 lb in weight from the Thames.

King James Way
King James I, in 1604, presented a Royal Charter to Henley that enabled the establishment of a Grammar School in the town. Although he provided some funding from the income of land and housing in the town, most had to come from elsewhere and was supplied by Augustine Knappe (see below) and later by William Gravett (above). A replica of the Charter is on display in the Town Hall.

Knappe Close
In his will of 1602, Augustine Knappe left £200 to the Corporation to support the foundation of a free Grammar School for 20 poor boys. This led the Corporation

104 *Archbishop William Laud who, in 1645, left funds to support Henley charities.*

to acquire the Chantry House and to invest some of the money in land and property in Henley and Remenham in order to provide a continuing income.

Lauds Close

William Laud was born in Reading in 1573 and became Archbishop of Canterbury in 1633. As a don at Oxford, he was a tutor to Bulstrode Whitelock and was President of St John's College in 1636. His attempts, as Archbishop, to coerce the Church of Scotland to adopt the doctrines and practices of the Church of England led to wars between Charles I and the Scottish Covenanters who, when the Civil War broke out, supported the Parliamentarian side. When the Long Parliament was formed after the defeat of Charles I, Archbishop Laud was arrested, found guilty and imprisoned. He was tried for treason over the role that he played in the recent political power struggles, found guilty and executed at Tower Hill in 1645. In his will he specified, among other things, that land with an annual rental value of £200 should be purchased and the income used by charitable trusts to pay £50 per year to each of the towns of Henley, Wokingham, Wallingford and New Windsor, in order to enable poor boys to be apprenticed and to provide gifts on the marriage of poor girls. As well as being poor, the parents of the recipients had to be 'true and faithful members of the Church of England'.

Lawson Road

Mr and Mrs David and Maureen Lawson were much involved for many years in running the Henley branch of the YMCA, Mrs Lawson acting as Honarary Secretary for 27 years. Some of the land from its sports field was sold to a Housing Trust to make way for the social housing that was built on Lawson Road and Noble Road in 2000 and an adjacent area was purchased for a new sports field. David Lawson was chairman of the branch at the time of his death in 1997.

Leaver Road

Ernest Leaver, who lived in Henley all his life, was treasurer to the Borough of Henley before the reorganisation of local government in 1974, and then Town Clerk from 1974 till 1983. It is reported that, at one time, he knew who lived at every house in the town.

Lovell Close

Lovell Close, where houses were built in about 1965, was named after Mrs Jessie Lovell, a town councillor who became the first woman Mayor of Henley in 1956 and Mayor again in 1961.

Luker Avenue

Charles Luker purchased Higgs & Co., the publishers of the *Henley Standard*, in 1900 when he was only 24, having come to Henley to learn the printing trade with Mr Higgs. At that time the paper was barely profitable, but he made the business successful again and ran it for many years. He was Editor-in-Chief of the *Henley Standard* for 60 years. During that time he was mayor on eight occasions, including the wartime period 1939-44 and also a County Councillor. He died in 1968, aged 91. His son Tom Luker became increasingly involved in the business and, as a result of his influence, the *Henley Standard*, instead of consistently supporting the Conservative Party as previously, became independent of party politics.

105 *Charles Luker (1876-1968), a long-term editor, manager and publisher of the* Henley Standard, *awarded an OBE in 1955.*

Makins Road

In 1872, the house known as Rotherfield Court was bought by Colonel William Makins, who was the MP for South Essex. The Colonel enlarged the house to incorporate a library and a billiard room and he also purchased several hundred acres of the adjoining land. Later he was created a baronet, becoming Sir William Makins. He became a magistrate, and also presented several stained glass windows to St Mary's Church. His son, Paul (1871-1939), who inherited the baronetcy in 1906, had acquired the house known as Chilterns End in Henley and, in 1911, was appointed as High Sheriff of Oxfordshire. During the First World War, Sir Paul Makins served as a major, and initially was appointed to make compulsory purchases of horses for the army from farmers and traders in the area. Subsequently he served in France. After the war, he lived at Rotherfield Court which, during the war, had been used as a hospital for injured army officers. At about this time, he donated several parcels of land for purposes such as road widening and the building of council houses at Rotherfield Greys. He also donated, in memory of his wife, the area known as the Makins Recreation Ground in Greys Road for public use. In 1923, Sir Paul Makins moved to London and the family's connection with the Henley area appears to have come to an end. Rotherfield Court, in 1928, became the home of Henley Grammar School.

Milton Close

Presumably named after John Milton (1608-74) who, as well as being an influential writer and poet, was a supporter of the Parliamentarians and of Oliver Cromwell. Milton Close was built, in 1969-70, on the site of the demolished Paradise House, and so there is a possible allusion to Paradise Lost. Paradise House was where Mary Blandy (see p.101) met William Cranston in about 1750, and was the home of William Brakspear from 1852 to 1882.

Nicholas Road

The origin of this name is uncertain but a Nicholas Field and a Nicholas Coppice were referred to in a deed of 1655, and an Edward Nicholas was referred to in a lease of some land in Henley in 1775. Nicholas Hill Farm, no longer a working farm, is about 250 yards to the north.

Noble Road

Members of the Noble family, who owned Park Place from 1872 till 1946, at one time also owned Harpsden Court and the land on which the houses of Noble Road have been built. John Noble, the first of his family to own Park Place, was the head of a business that manufactured paints and varnishes. Colonel Leonard Noble (1859-1943), who farmed at Harpsden Court Farm in the early 1900s, was High Sheriff of Oxfordshire in 1905. He provided Henley with a milk delivery service by ox cart.

Pearce's Orchard

This cul-de-sac occupies a site that was previously an orchard owned by a Mr Pearce, who lived at one of the large Oxford Villas on the Fair Mile.

Periam Close

Lady Elizabeth Periam was the sister of Sir Francis Bacon and her first husband was Richard D'Oyley, who lived at Greenlands. After his death, she inherited the house and estate. Her second husband, Sir Henry Neville, represented Queen Elizabeth at several European courts and her third husband was Sir William Periam, Lord Chief Baron of the Exchequer. As each marriage ended in widowhood for Lady Periam, the wealth that she acquired before her own death at Greenlands in 1621 was considerable. Partly due to the influence of William Laud, she became interested in promoting education, endowing Balliol College with a fellowship and two scholarships. In 1609 she founded and endowed a charity school in the lower floor of the Chantry House in Henley, where 20 poor local boys were to be given an education in 'writing, reading and casting of accounts' before being apprenticed. There is a full-sized effigy of Lady Periam in St Mary's Church that shows her reading a book.

Putman Close

Mr Joseph Putman, who lived in the house and shop that adjoins the present Close in Friday Street, was a maker and supplier of canvas tents and bags. A major fire in 1908 destroyed his storage premises and much of his stock. During the 1930s, he provided many of the tents and marquees that were used by the Regatta, and stored them during the rest of the year in outhouses at the rear of his premises. After his death in the late 1940s, squash courts were built on part of the site, and these have since been replaced by a group of town houses.

Ravenscroft Road

George Ravenscroft was one of the greatest English glassmakers, and several specimens of his glassware are on display at the Victoria and Albert Museum. He spent some years experimenting with fine crystalline glass in London before setting up a glassworks in

106   *The effigy of Lady Periam in St Mary's church.*

Henley in 1674. He was probably attracted to Henley by the fact that there was a good supply of silica in the local sands and flints, and there was also a plentiful supply of wood for the kilns. His main innovation was to add a lead flux to his glass which enabled him to guarantee it against 'crizzling', which caused the glass to become opaque. As a result of this improvement in quality, he was given permission to mark his products with a specific seal showing a raven's head. The location of his workshop is uncertain and a small archaeological dig at a possible site on the west side of Bell Street failed to find any evidence of its presence there. Although Ravenscroft died in 1681, the workshop in Henley continued for a few more years before ceasing production.

Rupert Close
Prince Rupert (1619-82), a grandson of James I and a nephew of Charles I, was a Royalist cavalry officer during the Civil War who, for several months, had his headquarters at the *Bell* inn at Northfield End. After the execution of Charles I, Prince Rupert turned to life as a pirate, attacking shipping off the south and west coasts until, with the restoration of Charles II, he returned to live in London.

Simmons Road
W. Anker Simmons was an auctioneer who had premises near the railway station and was later a partner in the firm of Simmons and Sons, surveyors. Together with Archibald Brakspear, he was part of a strong Masonic group on the Borough Council in the early 1900s. He was Mayor of Henley from 1905 to 1907, and received the Freedom of the Borough in 1921. The photograph of the Borough Council (p. 52) shows him, as Mayor, standing at the head of the table. He died in 1927.

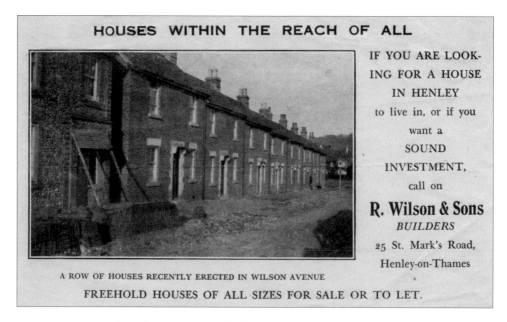

HOUSES WITHIN THE REACH OF ALL

IF YOU ARE LOOK-
ING FOR A HOUSE
IN HENLEY

to live in, or if you

want a

SOUND

INVESTMENT,

call on

R. Wilson & Sons
BUILDERS

25 St. Mark's Road,

Henley-on-Thames

A ROW OF HOUSES RECENTLY ERECTED IN WILSON AVENUE

FREEHOLD HOUSES OF ALL SIZES FOR SALE OR TO LET.

107 *An advertisement for houses in Wilson Avenue, c.1930.*

Singers Lane
Mr C.A. Singer came to Henley in 1868 and set up a grocery business in Duke Street. He was a town councillor from 1886 to 1904, mayor in 1891, and was responsible for the small paved area next to the *Angel*, now known as Singer's Park, being acquired by the Town Council.

Walton Avenue
Thought to be named after Percy Walton, who was appointed as a surveyor for Henley RDC in 1926 and remained in that post till 1951.

Wilson Avenue
Richard Wilson built a number of the Edwardian houses in St Mark's Road and elsewhere in the town, and later built the houses on the west side of Wilson Avenue. He was Mayor of Henley in 1918.

York Road
As York Road was developed, like Clarence Road, in about 1900, it is likely that it was named after the Duke of York who, like the Duke of Clarence, was a son of Edward VII and a grandson of Queen Victoria. Although the Duke of York was the second son, he outlived the Duke of Clarence and therefore, in due course, became King George V.

11

The History of Country Houses within three miles of Henley

Some of the large country houses in the area are the successors of manors that were in existence at the time of Domesday Book. Examples include Bolney Court, Fawley Court, Greys Court and Harpsden Court. However, in many instances the original building has been replaced or greatly modified and extended in later years. Other country houses were built at various times from the 1300s to the late 1800s, and again many have undergone changes. The earliest of the county maps, produced by Saxton in 1574, shows nine substantial parks in Oxfordshire, including Greys Court but not Henley Park, although the latter has been in existence since before 1300. The medieval parks, such as the one at Greys Court, were intended primarily to provide the landowner with an enclosed area for hunting deer without contravening the law that reserved all game in the wider countryside for the king. Although deer parks became less popular for hunting purposes after about 1700, they continued to be appreciated for their attractiveness, and many Oxfordshire parks, including those at Crowsley Park, Greys Court, Henley Park and Stonor Park, still had herds of deer in the 1800s. Stonor still does. Several of the local country houses now have the designation 'Court', a term that became fashionable and was adopted quite widely in the 1800s.

Sixteen country houses are described below, and although two of them, Friar Park and Phyllis Court, are now within the town boundary, they were outside the town at the time they were built, and they still have substantial grounds and much of the atmosphere of country houses. All 16 houses were privately owned and occupied, in some instances by tenants, in the early 1900s, but in 2007 two were occupied by golf or country clubs (Badgemore and Phyllis Court) and two by educational establishments (Greenlands and Shiplake College), one was owned by the National Trust (Greys Court), one by a religious community (Fawley Court), one was being run commercially as a venue for conferences and weddings (Bix Manor) and eight were still in private occupation though, in several instances, with much smaller estates than they had 100 years ago. One (Park Place) was unoccupied and its future is currently uncertain.

Badgemore

In the early 1700s, when Badgemore was just a farmhouse, the property was bought by Richard Jennings, who had been educated at the Lady Periam School in Henley and later worked as a master mason at St Paul's Cathedral. The Cathedral accounts contain the following entry for December 1706: 'To Richard Jennings: For his skill and extraordinary pains, care and diligence in the performance of the centering of the Dome and for modelling the same: fifty guineas'. After St Paul's had been completed in 1710, Jennings built a house (the present one) at Badgemore and lived there for several years.

He died in 1718 and was buried in St Mary's Church in Henley; there is a monument to him in the churchyard. The house at Badgemore, after being bought and sold several times, was acquired by Joseph Grote, a banker, who added the dining room and library in the 1780s. At that time, it was described as having about 40 acres of pleasure grounds. In 1833, Charles Lane purchased the estate and it remained in the Lane family till 1883 when it was bought by Richard Ovey, who also acquired the Hernes estate, between Henley and Rotherfield Greys, and became the High Sheriff for Oxfordshire. For a time during the Second World War, Badgemore was used to house German prisoners of war, and later the property was run as a riding stables. The house and surrounding grounds were sold in the 1970s and became the Badgemore Golf and Country Club.

Bix Manor

The main house of Bix Manor was built in 1670 but it was extended in the 1800s and again in the 1900s. One of the barns associated with the house dates from the 1600s. The house was part of the Stonor estate until it was sold, together with farmland, in 1894. In the late 1950s, the house became a private residence and the farmland was sold to the Nettlebed estate. The house and one of its associated barns, which has an unusual herring-bone pattern in its brickwork, now provide a venue for meetings, conferences and weddings.

Bolney Court

The estate around Bolney Court was owned by the Elmes family from the 1400s to about 1750, when it was bought by the Hodges family who had acquired plantations in the West Indies. Anthony Hodges (1755-81) died in St Kitts and his body was brought back for burial in Harpsden churchyard. The house was uninhabited for more than 30 years and became derelict, but was rebuilt in 1852 by Mr J.F. Hodges, who had become wealthy through his ownership of coal mines in Lancashire. Later, in the early 1900s, this house, too, was demolished to make way for the current house, which was built in 1912 and was described in sale particulars in 2006 as 'an idyllic and impressive Arts and Crafts country house' with 180 yards of river frontage but with only 12 acres of land.

Crowsley Park

A house at Crowsley Park was owned in 1685 by the Stonor family but they sold it, in 1701, to the Aldworth family who may well have built the present house. The park was enclosed and a herd of deer introduced as a visual attraction. By the early 1800s, the house and estate, which then amounted to about 2,400 acres, were owned by John Atkyns-Wright. He was the MP for Oxford, and he and his family lived at Crowsley in great style. After his death in 1822, his widow lived on at Crowsley until 1842, and the house was then bought by Henry Baskerville who had business interests in India. His son, Colonel John Baskerville, inherited the estate in 1877 and lived there until 1927.

In 1883, Colonel Baskerville hosted the Shiplake, Dunsden and Harpsden Flower Show, which was described in the following terms:

> Colonel Baskerville's beautiful Park, with its stately avenues can never have afforded a prettier sight than it did on this occasion. Besides the large marquee in which the main part of the Show was held, there were separate tents for specimens of needlework, for fruit,

for the exhibition of bees and for refreshment; the band of the Oxfordshire Hussars were present in uniform, and at a little distance a vigorous game of cricket was being fought out. The combination of the people's holiday with unbroken sunshine brought a large gathering together, not far short of a thousand, among whom it was pleasant to see all the children from the Henley Union Workhouse, whom Mrs Baskerville had very kindly invited.

Sir Arthur Conan Doyle was a friend of the Baskerville family, and although the setting of The Hound of the Baskervilles is in Devon, there are possible allusions to features of Crowsley Park. The Baskerville family hosted another special event in 1887 when they invited all parishioners to celebrate Queen Victoria's Golden Jubilee. However, Colonel Baskerville is reputed to have lost a large bet on a horse in 1904 and, as a result, much of the farmland in the estate was subsequently sold off. Crowsley Park itself was sold in 1927.

During the Second World War, Crowsley Park was requisitioned by the government, the deer were removed, and the parkland was, and is still, used by the BBC for the reception of overseas broadcasts. In the early 1990s the house, which had been unoccupied for many years, was sold and the new owners have since renovated the property and its surrounding gardens.

Culham Court

This large Georgian country house can be seen most clearly from the Thames path between Aston and Hurley. The house was built in 1771 for Robert Mitchell, an earlier house having been destroyed by fire. George III visited in 1804 and, while there, his host, the Hon. R. West, had his favourite hot rolls brought for him by horse from his baker in London. From the 1920s to the 1940s, the house was owned and rented out by Viscount Hambleden, and in the 1930s and 1940s it was occupied by the family of Cecil King, the newspaper magnate. During the war, Cecil King provided accommodation in the house for evacuee children from London. It was sold in 1948, again in 1997, and again, after complete renovation, in 2006. On the last occasion, it was advertised for sale together with 650 acres of land for a minimum price of £25 million.

Fawley Court

At the time of Domesday Book, the manor of Fawley was held by Walter Gifford, the Earl of Buckingham. Later, in the 1100s, the Sackville family built a fortified manor house on the site of the present Fawley Court and lived there until the late 1400s. In 1616, Fawley Manor, which at that time was probably a large medieval house, was purchased by Sir James Whitelock. He was a lawyer who was Commissioner of the Peace for Buckinghamshire and later for Oxfordshire as well but, despite these appointments, he favoured some curtailment of royalty's freedom of action. He was highly respected in Henley and on several occasions the Corporation presented him with gifts such as haunches of venison. After his death in 1632 and burial in Fawley church, King Charles I referred to him as 'a stout wise and learned judge'. His son, Sir Bulstrode Whitelock, inherited Fawley Court and Manor, and he also bought Phyllis Court and the title of the lord of the manor of Henley. At the time of the Civil War, Sir Bulstrode supported the Parliamentarian cause and fought in the army under Cromwell. However, Fawley Court was severely damaged by Royalist troops, who occupied it for a time. Subsequently, Sir Bulstrode Whitelock became Governor of Henley and was appointed by Cromwell to various posts which included being ambassador to Sweden. After

108   *Fawley Court, c.1900.*

the restoration of Charles II, he was heavily fined for his part in the Civil War, though it is possible that this was, at least partly, revoked. Sir Bulstrode retired to his house in Wiltshire and passed the ownership of the damaged Fawley Court to his eldest son James, but no repairs were carried out and in 1680 it was sold to a Colonel William Freeman.

Colonel Freeman had a new house (the present one) built in 1684, in a style made fashionable by Christopher Wren, who was a friend of his. Freeman had fought with Bulstrode Whitelock in the Civil War and had since become wealthy, particularly by trading in sugar from his estates, manned by slaves, in the West Indies. His wealth enabled him to have the house rebuilt, and to decorate and furnish it to a high standard, as well as improve the appearance of the grounds. Some of the interior decoration was carried out by Grinling Gibbons, and it is possible that 'Capability' Brown was involved in the landscaping of the parkland. Around 1770, Sambrooke Freeman, who had inherited the estate, bought the adjacent property of Phyllis Court. He also commissioned James Wyatt to create an appropriate summer house, and the result was the temple, just visible from Henley bridge, that gives its name to Temple Island. This project was part of a trend for the owners of country houses to create the appearance of natural landscapes in their estates and then to add 'picturesque' and classical features. Sambrook Freeman's enthusiasm for this style was probably gained during his travels in Italy, and was reinforced by his becoming a member of the Society of Arts. During his time at Fawley Court, it was the venue for many social events, including musical dinners organised by Mrs Freeman. Both George III and George IV visited the house on several occasions.

When Sambrook Freeman died, a nephew, Strickland Freeman, inherited the estate which then remained in the ownership of the Freeman family until it was sold in 1853 to Edward MacKenzie. He was a Scottish banker and his son, William D. Mackenzie (1840-1928), a surveyor and railway engineer, added the side wing to the house in 1884. He also created the canal-like waterway from the house to the Thames, planted more trees and restocked the deer park, but transferred the manorial rights of Henley manor to the Henley Corporation. His son, Major William R.D. MacKenzie, sold much of the estate in 1931-2 but remained owner of the house.

109   *Sambrook Freeman,*
owner of Fawley Court from
1752 to 1782.

110   *Temple Island, c.1930.*

During the Second World War the house was requisitioned by the army and used as a centre for training prospective undercover agents in wireless communication. Major MacKenzie was given only one week's notice to move out, and so hurriedly had to pack up his more valuable furniture and decorative items and store them in the basement and outbuildings. The army left the house in poor condition but Major MacKenzie returned and lived there until his death in 1952. The estate, including Henley Park, was then subdivided and put up for sale in a number of lots, but because of its size and condition the main house at Fawley Court was threatened with demolition. However, it was bought in 1953 by the Polish Congregation of Marian Fathers who founded a Catholic secondary school for boys, most of whom had parents of Polish origin. The school closed in 1986 and the Marian Fathers then converted the house for use as a religious retreat and conference centre. They also allocated some rooms for a museum, which includes items used by the Polish army in past centuries, together with a library containing historic Polish documents, early books and paintings.

Temple Island remained in the ownership of a member of the MacKenzie family until 1987, when a 999-year lease was purchased by the stewards of Henley Regatta, who had been given a private donation for the purpose. From 1894 till 1952, the small cottage attached to the temple was occupied by a caretaker and his wife. After 1987, the Regatta stewards had the temple renovated, a project that included the restoration of interior wall paintings based on scenes from the early excavations at Pompeii. The temple is now used for occasional dinners and receptions.

Friar Park

The present house at Friar Park, which has more than 100 rooms, was built in 1889-96 for Frank Crisp, a wealthy London solicitor who had an earlier house on the site demolished. Frank Crisp had rather eccentric tastes, and the house was designed by the

111   *The house at Friar Park built for the London lawyer, Frank Crisp, and completed in 1896.*

112   *The topiary garden at Friar Park.*

architect M. Clarke Edwards in a showy Gothic style with towers and bay windows, somewhat resembling a French chateau. It had several quirky features. For example, images of friars were used to decorate the light switches inside the house, and the lights were switched on by the moveable noses. There were also gargoyles in the shape of friars on the roof outside. The name of the house and the choice of friars as a decorative theme reflect the earlier name of Friar's Field for the land on which it stands. Frank Crisp also spent a great deal of money and time on the grounds. His gardens, which took 20 years to complete to his satisfaction, included not only herbaceous, alpine, Japanese and topiary gardens but also 25 glasshouses, a maze and two huge rock gardens, including a replica of the Matterhorn 100 feet high. More than 7,000 tons of rock were obtained from Yorkshire for the rock garden. A bridge over the lower of two lakes was positioned so that anyone who crossed it would appear from the house to be walking on water. Under the rock gardens were caves, known as the 'Blue Grotto of Capri' and the 'Ice Caves of Grunewald', which incorporated underground lakes lit by electricity. According to a book by Judy Slinn, the Blue Grotto contained a model of a Chinese stork which drank water from the lake when a button was pushed, and there were, in addition, a vine

113 *The miniature replica of the Matterhorn in the rock gardens at Friar Park, c.1920.*

cave with glass grapes, a skeleton cave, an illusion cave with optical trickery and a gnome cave. Favoured visitors could paddle through the lakes in a swan-shaped boat.

The grounds extended as far as Northfield End, and Frank Crisp had his own boathouse built by the river at Wharfe Lane – the house now known as Waters Edge. He also built six pairs of cottages in the road known as Hop Gardens for his estate workers. On Wednesday afternoons from May to September he opened the grounds of Friar Park to the public and, in 1910, he wrote a *Guide for Use of Visitors to Friar Park*, a book of 280 pages in which he explained his eccentric approach to the design of the house and gardens. After his death in 1919 the property was sold, but subsequent owners found it difficult to maintain. For several years it was divided into apartments and then, from 1953 to 1970, it was owned by the Salesian Sisters, a Catholic order of nuns. For part of that time it was used as a school. Maintenance became increasingly expensive and, as the nuns were unable to raise the necessary finance, it was threatened with demolition in 1969-70. At this point, George Harrison, of the Beatles, appeared on the scene, looking for a home that would provide a combination of privacy and space, and with easy access to London. He was attracted to the house with its eccentricities, and bought it. Over the next few years he spent a large amount of money restoring both the house and the gardens. George Harrison also installed what were then the most sophisticated private recording studios in the world and, as part of his album All Things Must Pass, he composed and recorded a song entitled 'The Ballad of Sir Frankie Crisp'. For a time during the 1970s, Harrison housed a group of his friends from the Hare Krishna movement at Friar Park. Unfortunately for the public, he considered it necessary to adopt tight security precautions with all public access prohibited and razor wire placed above the fences around the estate. These precautions, however, failed to prevent a night-time intruder entering the house and seriously wounding George Harrison in 1999. Since his death, in 2004, the house has continued in the ownership of his family. Opinions on the merits of the house have varied widely. Cecil Roberts referred to it in 1935 as a 'monstrous spikey palace', but in 1990 it was described in the *Sunday Times* as 'a beautiful example of high Victorian architecture in the style of Pugin'.

The lodge and gateway at the entrance of Friar Park on Gravel Hill give some impression of the architectural style of the main house which is now hidden by trees in the surrounding parkland.

114 *Greenlands as it was in 1914.*

Greenlands

Until 1480, Greenlands was part of the Stonor estate. The original house was nearer to Hambleden village than the present one, though still close to the river, and was known as the Manor of Greenland. It was purchased from Sir William Stonor by John D'Oyley, who owned the neighbouring estate of Yewden Manor, and the D'Oyley family remained there until the Civil War. Early in the war, Greenlands was occupied by Royalist troops who tried to prevent the transport of food and other supplies by river to the Parliamentary forces in London. Despite being well fortified, the house was bombarded from across the river by Parliamentarian troops, and the Royalists were eventually forced to surrender. Substantial amounts of ammunition from the Civil War have since been found in the vicinity.

After the war, in 1651, John D'Oyley sold the ruined house and the manor of Greenland to his neighbour Sir Bulstrode Whitelock, who already owned Fawley Court and Phyllis Court. Sir Bulstrode then owned all the riverside land on the north-west side of the Thames between Henley and Mill End. However, in 1660 the Greenlands estate, still without a habitable house, was sold again and some years later a farmhouse was built. Around 1810 the estate was bought by Thomas Darby-Coventry, who built a new house. The next sale, in 1853, was to Edward Marjoribanks MP, who had been renting Fawley Court from the Freeman family, and Mr Marjoribanks extended the house into a substantial mansion. He was responsible for the layout of the grounds, planting many of the specimen trees of various types, including oaks, cedars and maples, that are still there.

The next owner in 1872 was W.H. (William Henry) Smith who had greatly expanded the family newsagency business started by his father, rather confusingly called H.W. (Henry Walton) Smith. William Henry Smith had become wealthy, mainly by gaining an exclusive right to sell newspapers from bookstalls at all the major railway stations in England. He was later elected as an MP and, in Disraeli's government, became First Lord of the Admiralty and Leader of the House of Commons. He was widely respected for his integrity. While W.H. Smith lived there, Greenlands was a family house with a large domestic staff, where entertaining and house parties were regular features. For some years, there were about thirty gardeners on the staff. After his death, aged 66, in 1891, his widow Emily Smith was granted the title of Viscountess Hambleden by Queen Victoria, and she continued to live at Greenlands. Her son, William Danvers Smith, the 2nd Viscount Hambleden (taking into account his mother's peerage), ran the estate until he died in 1928, when he was succeeded by his son, the 3rd Viscount. Although workers on the estate in the 1920s and early 1930s had no holidays, other than Bank Holidays, they did have security of employment, a pension and a house for life. A one-week holiday was introduced in the late 1930s.

In 1939, part of Greenlands was relinquished by the 3rd Viscount for occupation by 30 adult evacuees from a home in London who stayed until the end of the war. In 1947, Viscount Hambleden and his family moved to the Manor House in Hambleden village, and the house at Greenlands was at first leased and then bought by the Administrative Staff College, which became the Henley Management College and now has an international reputation for training senior business managers.

Greys Court

In the years after 1066, Greys Court was held by a Norman family, the de Greys. The family gained royal favour during the reign of Edward I (1272-1307) when Sir Robert de Grey made an important contribution to Edward's defeat of the Welsh, and in 1344 Sir John Grey was authorised to build fortifications on his property in recognition of his participation in the Battle of Crecy. The house, as it then existed, was incorporated into one side of a square enclosure with circular towers at each corner. A descendant of Sir John was killed in the Battle of Bosworth, and after that the ownership of Greys Court reverted to King Henry VII. Later, in about 1515, Henry VIII granted it to one of his courtiers, whose son became Sir Francis Knollys. Sir Francis was a good friend of Henry VIII and, after Henry's death, became an adviser to Elizabeth I who, as a result,

115   *Greys Court (Photograph 1973).*

often visited Greys Court. The Knollys family built the present Elizabethan manor house, which remained in their possession until 1688, when it was acquired, through marriage, by the Stapleton family. The Stapletons extended the house in the 1750s and it continued in the ownership of their descendants until 1935.

Sir Felix and Lady Brunner purchased Greys Court in 1937, at which time the buildings comprised the Elizabethan house together with a tower that had survived from 1347. The Brunners were responsible for developing the gardens as they now exist, apparently gaining inspiration from those at Sissinghurst in Kent. In 1969, they transferred the property, including 290 acres of woodland and pasture, to the National Trust. Since then, as well as maintaining the gardens, which include a wisteria arbour and ornamental vegetable plots, the Trust has restored an old ice house and installed a maze constructed of brick pathways. Inspiration for the maze is reported to have come from the enthronement speech of Dr Robert Runcie as Archbishop of Canterbury in 1980.

Hambleden Manor

In the 1400s, Hambleden manor belonged to the Earl of Gloucester. The present manor house was built around 1604 for a nobleman who became the Earl of Sutherland but, in 1651, it was sold to Sir Bulstrode Whitelock. He was followed by a succession of owners. The manor house was the birthplace, in 1797, of the Earl of Cardigan who led the Charge of the Light Brigade in the Crimean War, and is also said to have invented the woolly cardigan. During the 1800s and early 1900s, the house and estate were owned by the Scott-Murray family, and the house was altered and enlarged in about 1830. Much of their land was later sold to W.H. Smith, who had already acquired the estate at Greenlands. Hambleden manor itself was later purchased by the 3rd Viscount Hambleden, who moved there with his family from Greenlands in 1947.

Harpsden Court

Domesday Book records Harpsden Court as being occupied by a Saxon named Alured, whose son later adopted the Norman name of Roger de Harpeden and built the church nearby. The Forster family lived there for about 200 years from the mid-1400s and, in 1586, Humphrey Forster commissioned John Blagrave of Reading to produce a map of Harpsden manor. The map, part of which is reproduced in the book, *The Chilterns*, by Hepple and Doggett, shows several lanes and a number of field boundaries that have survived almost unchanged to the present time. However, there was considerably more land under arable cultivation in 1586 than at the present time. The Forsters sold the estate and the lordship of the Manor of Harpsden in 1646 to General Bartholomew Hall, who was a friend of Bulstrode Whitelock and of Oliver Cromwell.

The Hall family continued to live at Harpsden during the 1700s, and Thomas Hall, who inherited the property from his father, a lawyer, in 1747, was the first member of his family to become a country gentleman. He modified the house to incorporate a music room and supper room, both of which were decorated with rococo plaster-work. Like some of his predecessors, Thomas Hall sympathised with the nonconformists in terms of religion even though he attended Harpsden church. He supported the Independent Chapel in Henley and was a friend of Humphrey Gainsborough who was then the minister there.

Until about 1800 the house had four courts, but it was then reduced to its present size in a partial demolition that removed 34 rooms. In 1855, Harpsden Court was purchased

116   *Harpsden Court.*
(Photograph, 2006)

by Mr J.F. Hodges of Bolney Court, but he continued to live at Bolney Court. From 1897 till 1976 it belonged to the Noble family who were based at Park Place and, in the 1930s, Colonel Leonard Noble opened the grounds to the public every Sunday. When the house was sold in 1976, it was sold separately from most of its park and farmland. It is now privately owned but is used from time to time as a setting for television films.

Henley Park

Henley Park dates from the medieval period, though the present house, possibly the smallest of those described in this Chapter, was built in the late 1800s. The first written reference to Henley Park appears to be in 1300, when it was mentioned in an inquisition relating to the death of the Earl of Cornwall. It had a succession of owners before being bought in 1620 by Sir James Whitelock (father of Sir Bulstrode) who, four years previously, had bought Fawley Court. In 1662, a house at Henley Park was being rented by a Dr Cawley, the rector of Henley. In 1672, a William Whitelock of Fawley Court (one of Sir Bulstrode's sons) obtained a licence to fell much of the woodland in the Park and convert the land to arable or pasture. A few years later, both Henley Park and Fawley Court were bought by Colonel William Freeman, and in 1731 a John Freeman buried a time capsule near the highest point of the Mount in Henley Park. For many years, an earthwork there was thought to be a prehistoric burial mound but an excavation in 1932 uncovered the capsule together with a piece of glass on which the following inscription was written in Latin, apparently with the use of a diamond:

> In the year of Our Lord 1731, John Freeman of Fawley has raised up this mass mound having buried in it a medley of pieces of glass of vessels of pottery and other household utensils and furniture, so that, if perchance at some time some curious posterity should examine this old rubbish, it may find something to give pleasure and perhaps profit since some arts are dying out … The fields of the surrounding district are sown with wheat, barley, pease, oats, pulse, beans and grass. The hills on each side are clothed with woods, chiefly composed of beech, ash and oak and in most of the gardens are elms. In the gardens of Fawley is planted every kind of tree which is known in Europe …

The capsule contained various items including examples of Japanese porcelain, early English lead crystal glass, earthenware and wine bottles. Many of these items and the Latin inscription are now on display in the River & Rowing Museum.

When the wife of Sambrook Freeman was widowed, she decided in 1782 to move to the house at Henley Park rather than stay at Fawley Court. The house was then known as her dower house until she died in 1806 and it was leased out again. In 1804, a brick and flint wall along the Fair Mile from Northfield End to Lower Assenden was built to mark the boundary of Henley Park. However, after its completion, Strickland Freeman was indicted for blocking the public footpath from Northfield End to Fawley, and was made to reinstate the path by making a gap in the wall. More openings for various entrances have since been made in the wall but most of it is still intact, though some of the brick and flint-work is beginning to crumble. In the 1840s and early 1850s, the house was occupied by a Mr Newell Birch who provided the village school at Lower Assendon. Henley Park remained, with Fawley Court, in the ownership of the Freeman family until 1853, when both properties were sold to Edward McKenzie. The house at Henley Park was rebuilt by the MacKenzies in the late 1800s, and stayed in their ownership until 1953. The whole estate was then split into a number of separate lots before being sold again.

Park Place

Park Place was built in 1719-20, in the style of a French chateau, for Lord Archibald Hamilton. He became an MP and was subsequently appointed to be Lord of the Admiralty. The estate was sold in 1738 to Frederick Prince of Wales, the eldest son of George II, who lived there with the Princess of Wales until he died in 1751. The Princess then sold the estate to General Henry Conway (1721-95), the second son of Lord Conway. General Conway was an MP from 1747 to 1784, a government minister from 1764 to 1768, and a colleague of William Pitt the Elder. Despite these commitments in Parliament, he continued with his career in the army and later, in the 1780s, became the Governor of Jersey. General Conway was also prominent in local affairs, being a member of the Henley-Maidenhead Turnpike Trust and a Thames Commissioner. In addition he was a member of the Henley

117   *Park Place as it was in 1814.*

Bridge Commissioners, who arranged for the design and building of the bridge that was completed in 1786. General Conway spent much time and money enhancing both the house and estate at Park Place, thus impressing the guests who came to his dinners and house parties. As a result of his connections with the aristocracy and his role in the government, his guests included prominent people of several nationalities. Members of the French aristocracy often came to Park Place, but many of them lost their lives in the French Revolution.

General Conway employed Humphrey Gainsborough in 1763 in planning the construction of 'Conway's Bridge' over the so-called 'Happy Valley', a bridge that still forms part of the Wargrave Road. The bridge is thought to include stone reclaimed from the demolished Reading Abbey, and to have been constructed by ex-soldiers who had served under Conway in the army but who were otherwise unemployed. In 1768, he commissioned Humphrey Gainsborough again, on a major engineering project to reduce the slope of White Hill. This made it easier and less hazardous to travel in both directions, and took the road

118   *General Conway, a sketch based on a painting by Thomas Gainsborough.*

further from the house at Park Place. Another scheme that he introduced was the cultivation of about twenty acres of lavender on land at the bottom of the hill, and then distillation of the flowers to produce lavender oil. General Conway was also reputed to have planted the first Lombardy poplar tree in England, a cutting having been brought from Turin.

When he resigned from the governorship of Jersey, the island's inhabitants presented him with a 'Druids' Temple', which resembled a small version of Stonehenge and previously stood on a hill near St Helier. However, it had been hidden under a mound until the site was levelled. It consisted of a circle of 45 granite stones, about seven feet in height, and these were transported by sea and river to Park Place and erected in the grounds. General Conway also commissioned Humphrey Gainsborough's brother, the artist Thomas Gainsborough, to paint portraits of himself and his family.

Following the death of General Conway in 1795, his widow sold Park Place to Lord Malmesbury, who was a friend of the Prince Regent, later George IV. During the Napoleonic wars, Lord and Lady Malmesbury supported the formation of a temporary force of military volunteers, the Loyal Henley Association, a force that was later superseded by the Henley and Binfield Volunteers commanded by Major John Atkyns-Wright of Crowsley Park. In 1815, Lord Malmesbury auctioned the estate in various lots at Henley Town Hall. By 1837, the house and surrounding grounds were owned by Mr Fuller Maitland, who somehow acquired the top section (about thirty feet) of the spire from St Bride's Church, London, which had been struck by lightning in 1764. He then arranged for it to be transported to Park Place and mounted on a plinth to commemorate the accession of Queen Victoria. It is still there, close to the much more recently erected TV mast. Mr Maitland also improved both the house and grounds, and built the boathouse. In 1867, Park Place was bought as a speculation by Charles Easton of Whiteknights Park, Reading, and he sold it three years later to John Noble who was

119 *A plaque installed alongside the Druids' Temple at Park Place.*

a manufacturer of paints and varnishes. Soon afterwards, much of the interior of the house was destroyed by a fire, but John Noble had it restored and also built a stable block and planted thousands of specimen trees in the grounds. In 1905, Percy Noble compiled a book, *Park Place, Berkshire*, describing the history of the estate and many of its previous owners. The book was issued for 'private circulation' but a copy is available for reference in the Reading Borough Library. The property stayed in the ownership of the Noble family until 1946, when it was auctioned in 28 lots at Henley Town Hall.

The house was bought by Middlesex County Council who, from 1947, used it to accommodate 'delicate children who would benefit from the fresh air'. It was transferred to Hillingdon Council in 1965, again for use as a school but for children with behavioural difficulties. After this school closed in 1988, the house was bought by a Greek shipping billionaire but, although he re-purchased much of the land that formed the earlier estate, he left the house unoccupied. Aspect Park Golf Club was established on part of the area in the 1980s and continued till 2005. Executors sold the estate in 2004 to a consortium of businessmen who planned to restore the house and grounds, build additional housing and set up an exclusive country club. However their proposals were not acceptable to the planning authority and, in 2007, the house and estate were sold to a property company specialising in the development of luxury homes.

Phyllis Court

The area around Phyllis Court was the site of a small medieval manor known as Fillets (see p.9) that was granted to John de Molyns in 1347. After many changes in ownership, Filletts Court was bought, together with Henley Park, in 1638 by Sir Bulstrode Whitelock whose main residence was Fawley Court. When, during the Civil War, the Parliamentarians re-occupied Henley in 1643, men from Cromwell's army fortified Phyllis Court by building a wall at the riverside. Part of this is still visible. After the war, the damaged house was rebuilt and it continued in the ownership of the Whitelock family until it was sold in 1724. William of Orange was welcomed at Phyllis Court by William and Mary Whitelock in 1688 on his journey from Torbay in Devon to London to claim the throne of England. In 1768, Phyllis Court was bought by Sambrook Freeman of Fawley Court, and he rented

120   *Phyllis Court.*
(Photograph, 2006)

it to tenants. In 1777 it was occupied by a Lord Villiers who organised a Gala Week for the local gentry and their friends. A grand ball was held at Fawley Court with the support of Mr and Mrs Sambrook Freeman, and the guests are reported to have included the Duke of Argyll, a count and ten lords. The Gala Week also included performances of two plays in a temporary 300-seat theatre that had been installed in stables at Bolney Court.

Among others who took part in Henley's social scene in the years up to and around 1800 were the Conways of Park Place, the Freemans of Fawley Court and the Grotes of Badgemore. The two lodges by Phyllis Court Drive were built in the early 1800s by Strickland Freeman, who had inherited both Fawley Court and Phyllis Court. In the 1830s, the house was rebuilt in its present style as a large two-storey villa by Admiral Williams-Freeman, who had inherited it from Strickland Freeman. The Henley Horticultural Society held its shows in the grounds. Phyllis Court, together with Fawley Court, was sold at auction in 1853 to Edward MacKenzie. Some years later, in 1884, Mr MacKenzie was concerned, on behalf of his tenants, about the number of house boats moored by the river bank at Phyllis Court. He complained to the Parliamentary Select Committee on River Thames Preservation in the following terms:

> The use of houseboats has been extending very much during the last three or four years. They now come up the river and place themselves in certain positions and remain there for the whole of the summer ... They pay the Conservators no toll whatever, unless they go through a lock ... There are at present 23, extending from above Phyllis Court downward, beside 16 launches. The houseboats are higher than the bank. Phyllis Court has a beautiful terrace walk along the river, but during this fortnight the tenant of that place is debarred from the pleasant use of his grounds ...

His comments had the desired effect and the Thames Conservators later prohibited houseboats from 'loitering' on specified sections of the river, most of them by the estates of wealthy landowners.

During the early 1900s, Phyllis Court was unoccupied for a few years though, each summer, the grounds were rented by the Regatta Stewards who installed an enclosure and marquees for visitors. Fireworks and illuminations there were part of the Regatta celebrations. In 1906, Phyllis Court was purchased, with the support of his parents, by Roy Finlay who

*121   House boats
on the Thames
near Henley,
c.1900.*

*122   The lawns at Phyllis
Court in Edwardian times.*

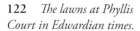

was then only 24 but had the intention of founding an upmarket social club. This project was successful and, in 1913, a grandstand in Edwardian style was erected on the riverbank to provide club members with a better view of the Regatta. The grandstand has recently been restored. During the First World War, Finlay served as a captain in the Dragoon Guards, but the club remained open. It became increasingly popular in the 1920s and '30s, and ownership of the premises was transferred to the Phyllis Court Members Club in 1937. During the Second World War, the main building was requisitioned for war use, first as a mess room for WAAF officers working at the Central Photographic Unit at RAF Medmenham, and then to house a secret unit for making maps and models from aerial photographs. This unit concentrated on the coastal areas of France where it was planned to land British and American troops in 1944. Phyllis Court later became a convalescent home for US airforce personnel. The Phyllis Court Club, whose activities had been suspended, re-opened in 1946. It regained its pre-war popularity but, during the night of Christmas Eve 1976, suffered a fire which badly damaged many of the rooms including the lounge and ballroom, and was subsequently found to have been caused by arson. However, Phyllis Court was restored and refurbished, and yet further improvements have since been carried out.

123 *Phyllis Court dining room with tables set for luncheon in Edwardian times.*

Shiplake Court (College)

The area where Shiplake College now stands has been occupied for at least seven hundred years. In the 14th century, Shiplake Court and its estate belonged to the Englefield family, whose ownership continued until Queen Elizabeth I confiscated all the land owned by Sir Francis Englefield. However, Shiplake Court was later leased to Sir Edmund Plowden and his family who, like the Englefields, were Catholics, and during the Civil War the house was plundered by Parliamentarian troops led by General Bartholomew Hall. Although the Plowden family was able to re-occupy the house after the war, they left in 1688 and it was subsequently bought by the Jennings family. In the late 1700s, the owner was bankrupted by gambling debts and the house was allowed to deteriorate. It was sold in 1802 and the house itself was then demolished and the grounds were incorporated into Shiplake Court Farm. As the popularity of Shiplake increased after the construction of the railway, the property was bought in 1888 by Mr Robert Harrison, a city stockbroker, who rebuilt the house as a Tudor-style mansion and also landscaped the grounds. Shiplake Court was bought by the BBC in 1941 to house staff involved in the monitoring of overseas broadcasts and centred at Caversham Park near Reading. On being sold by the BBC in 1958, it was bought by Mr and Mrs Alec Everett who converted the house into a boarding college for teenage boys, mainly those whose parents were working overseas. Shiplake College was duly opened in May 1959 and is now an independent day and boarding school for boys aged 13-18, with girls in the sixth form.

Wargrave Manor

The house known as Wargrave Manor is on the hillside overlooking the Thames and was built around 1790. It was originally called Wargrave Hill. The first manor house was almost certainly on the site where the house known as Wargrave Court now stands. During the 1800s, the present Wargrave Manor was owned by the Jekyll family and, from 1868, it was occupied by the parents of Gertrude Jekyll and their family. The house was named Wargrave Manor by Sir William Cain, who bought it in 1918. Since the mid-1970s it has been owned by the Sultan of Oman and occupied by a member of his family, and a herd of fallow deer has been introduced into the parkland.

12

Changes in the Surrounding Countryside and Villages

The attractiveness of the countryside around Henley is due to three main features, the River Thames, the Chiltern Hills and the surrounding villages. The Thames, with its towpath, has long been accessible to walkers for much of its length, and the towpath now forms part of a long-distance Thames Path which follows the river as closely as possible from its source near Lechlade to London. Of the villages within about three miles of Henley, several have retained much of their character from past centuries, their older buildings showing little change externally. Hambleden, which is unusual for a village of its size in still having both a pub and a shop, is the best example.

The importance of conserving the landscape of the Chilterns has been recognised at least since the 1930s, and in 1964 much of the area was designated an Area of Outstanding Natural Beauty. In this context, the definition of 'natural beauty' is not based entirely on scenery but takes into account the flora and fauna, the geology and the cultural heritage of the area. The Chilterns AONB covers an area of 325 square miles and extends from Goring and Mapledurham in the south-west to near Dunstable in the north-east. Although the main built-up area of Henley is not included in the AONB, some of the outer parts of the parish are included. The Chiltern Society which was founded in 1965 has been, and continues to be, active in supporting the objectives of the AONB designation, for example by encouraging high standards of planning in the area, and by maintaining footpaths and bridleways in good condition. All its work is carried out or funded by volunteers. In 2004, an official Chilterns Conservation Board was established, with the aims of conserving and enhancing the natural beauty of the Chilterns, and promoting a more co-ordinated approach amongst the various groups involved. Its membership includes representatives of local councils (including South Oxfordshire District Council) and several individuals appointed by DEFRA.

While the countryside on the Berkshire side of the river is not in the Chilterns and therefore not in the AONB, it has been, and still is, protected by the Metropolitan Green Belt. This has included, as part of its outer ring, the portion of Wokingham District to the north and east of Twyford but excluding the village of Wargrave.

Land Use

Even within a few miles of Henley, land use varies widely. Arable farming, livestock production, deciduous woodland, conifer plantations, parkland, golf courses and, increasingly, paddocks for horses, are all significant. Each of these uses, apart from golf courses, has been in existence for several centuries but their relative importance has changed. In early medieval times, much of the land immediately surrounding Henley appears to have been cultivated on the three-field system as indicated by the persistence of the names Northfield (in Northfield End), Westfield (in Westfield House, now demolished) and Southfield (in Southfield infants school, also now demolished). Individual peasants had their own strips of land but seasonal jobs such as ploughing, sowing and harvesting were planned and carried out jointly by the community. However, by the late 1500s, land holdings in the large open fields of many small towns and villages were, by general agreement, being amalgamated and enclosed to make management easier. In particular, enclosure made it more feasible to keep sheep for wool production. On hillier land such as the Chilterns, the three-field system was always less widespread, and the more usual form of agriculture was for small fields, obtained originally by clearing areas of woodland, to be managed by farming families acting independently.

By 1586, the map of Harpsden Manor mentioned on p. 122 shows that there were many small enclosed fields and many more individual farm holdings than at the present time. The map indicates that six individual farmers each had between seven and 13 fields within the manor; and when Siberechts painted his view of Henley in 1698 he showed the land surrounding the town to be occupied mainly by small enclosed fields with a mixture of arable cultivation and pasture.

After about 1730, it was possible for unenclosed land within a parish to be enclosed by order of an Act of Parliament, subject to approval by the Enclosure Commissioners who would decide on the allocation of land where there were disputes over ownership. Parliamentary enclosures occurred in some of the villages around Henley, for example in Binfield Heath and Rotherfield Greys. Although the enclosures improved agricultural productivity, villagers without appreciable land suffered. They lost their previous rights to graze cattle on common land, to collect wood for domestic use and to glean the grain left in the fields after harvesting. Some were then tempted to turn to poaching as a way of feeding their families, but this trend was met by Parliament introducing drastic punishments, and by landowners aquiring the authority to set man traps.

During the 1800s, and until about 1950, small farms, though tending to increase in size through amalgamation, continued to dominate the countryside around Henley. The types of crop being grown also showed relatively little change, and there was little change, until tractors replaced horses, in the methods of cultivation and harvesting. In the 1820s, for example, most of the agricultural land was being farmed on either a four- or a five-year rotation, and records from Rotherfield Greys show that the major crops were wheat, barley, oats, turnips, mustard and hay. Most farms produced a mixture of arable crops and livestock, the livestock production being designed to satisfy local demands for milk and meat, with wool being sent to London and elsewhere.

Since the 1940s, the proportion of the Henley area occupied by productive agriculture has declined and so have the number of farm holdings. The changes have been due, in part, to the conversion of farmland to housing and to leisure activities such as golf, in part to the economic difficulties of small farms, and in part to the effects of European agricultural policies. Arable crops are now grown mainly in large fields on large farms, such as those between Remenham Hill and Cockpole Green. Livestock production, especially dairy farming, has become much less widespread and more specialised, though there are still dairy farms at Shiplake and at Mill End near Hambleden, and beef cattle and sheep are reared at several farms near Henley.

The area occupied by woodland has undergone relatively little change in the past 100 years and probably in the past 300 years. There was a period in the latter half of the

124   *Haymaking in fields by Dairy Lane, Hambleden, early 1900s.*

1600s when considerable tree felling occurred, with some woodland being converted to agricultural use and some allowed to regenerate as woodland. More recently, during the period 1920-70, there was a trend for deciduous woodland to be replaced by conifers but these conifers, as they reach maturity, are now being replaced mainly by deciduous species. This change reflects a shift in government policy from encouraging the production of softwood timber to encouraging the planting of deciduous woodlands for landscape, wildlife and recreational purposes, as well as for timber. This policy will, of course, take many years to be fully implemented. Another change in Chiltern woodlands is the gradual but continuing replacement of beech by other deciduous species such as oak, ash and cherry. One reason for this is that many of the beech woods now in existence were planted about 100-150 years ago, when there was a large demand for beech timber (now greatly diminished) for furniture making at High Wycombe. Such trees, if not already felled, are now reaching the end of their life. However, during the last 70 years, many young replacement beech trees, either growing naturally from seed or planted, have been seriously damaged by grey squirrels which strip the bark from young trees.

From a scenic point of view, the Henley area is fortunate to have retained several areas of well-established parkland associated with some of the large country houses described in Chapter 10. All of the parklands have, of course, been subject to changes of use, in some instances by partial conversion to more intensive agriculture and, in two instances, by incorporating a golf course, but several still have areas of open grassland enhanced by mature trees. There was a surge in the number of golf courses in the area during the 1980s, and in 2005 there were five courses either wholly or partly within three miles of Henley.

Since 1960, two wildlife reserves have been officially designated within a few miles of Henley. The larger of the two is the Warburg Nature Reserve at Bix Bottom, a mainly woodland area that is owned and managed by the Berkshire, Buckinghamshire and Oxfordshire Wildlife Trust. The reserve, which is named after the Oxford botanist Dr E.F. Warburg, was purchased in 1968 with funds raised by an appeal to the public, largely organised by Mrs Vera Paul, who was at one time a teacher at Henley Grammar School. The other reserve is an area of marshy grassland and alder woodland at Temple Island Meadows near Fawley Court that has been designated by English Nature as a Site of Special Scientific Interest, partly due to the presence of the rather rare Loddon lily. Both Lambridge Wood and Harpsden Wood also have SSSI status, and were so designated in order to maintain their character as areas of ancient woodland.

A nationally uncommon bird that is prominent in, or at least over, Henley is the red kite which, having been almost eliminated from the UK by Victorian gamekeepers, was re-introduced to the south Chilterns in 1989. By 2005, numbers had increased to an estimated 300 breeding pairs in and around the Chilterns, and as many as 10-15 are sometimes visible circling over the town at one time.

Binfield Heath

The village of Binfield Heath is thought to have originated in Saxon times, probably as a result of the inhabitants of hamlets near the Thames moving to higher ground at times when the river flooded. The area around Binfield Heath would have provided a drier though less fertile area and would have been better for grazing animals when the land near the river was waterlogged. The temporary settlement gradually became a village in its own right, but with rather scattered cottages around a large area of open common land. This pattern continued till the mid-1800s, by which time the village was large enough to support three pubs. The village and its surroundings still held a considerable amount of common land, which was mainly poor grazing partially covered by gorse, but this was enclosed in the mid-1800s, partly by Robert Phillimore of Coppid Hall and partly by Henry Baskerville of Crowsley Park. Subsequently, the Baskervilles sold their land to the Phillimores.

The growth of Binfield Heath from the late 1800s onwards was encouraged when brick works were opened at Kiln Lane in about 1869, an industry that continued till 1935. Although still a rather scattered village, a chestnut tree and a shop now indicate its centre. For many years, Binfield Heath was in the parish of Shiplake, but in 2003 it was incorporated into a new civil parish of Binfield Heath with Crowsley. When it was part of Shiplake parish, the Anglican parishioners were expected to attend the church in Shiplake, but from 1835 a Congregational Chapel, built in mock-Tudor style in Binfield Heath itself, offered an alternative.

Bix

Bix is a village that is hardly noticed as one drives along the A4130 Henley-Oxford road. It now has no shop, pub or post office but it does have several features of interest. Two of these are easily seen. One is the dual carriageway of Bix Hill, one of the first dual-carriageways in the country, which was constructed as early as 1935-8, with space for a line of shrubs between the carriageways. At the time, it was envisaged as the first stage in a proposed by-pass for Henley that would run across the Mount, over the Thames and connect with the Henley to London road near the *Black Boy* at Hurley. A second feature is the toll house on the roadside in the village itself, dating from the time when the road was turnpiked. Toll houses had distinctive bay frontages that allowed the keeper to see the road in both directions, and this example has retained its original appearance externally. It was, for a number of years until the late 1960s, the village post office.

125   *The toll house at Bix, with its bay frontage giving a view of the road in both directions as typical in toll houses. (Photograph, 2006)*

A less obvious feature of the village is the restored Victorian water tank that was installed in the 1890s, alongside the lane to Broadplat, near its junction with the main road. The tank was unusual in being lined with bricks rather than clay, the bricks being obtained from the nearby Nettlebed brickworks. It filled naturally with rainwater and was intended primarily to provide a supply of water for steam engines, especially for the traction engines climbing Bix Hill on the Henley-Oxford road, and also those used for ploughing on the Nettlebed estate. The water tank also provided, through the operation of a hand pump, water for horses and for domestic use. As with other villages on the tops of the Chiltern ridges, Bix was vulnerable to a severe shortage of water during prolonged dry weather, and it was only in 1924-5 that a piped water supply arrived in Bix and Nettlebed. The water tank continued to be used for steam engines, but when they finally became redundant in the 1950s it became derelict. It was restored by volunteers from the Chiltern Society in 2002. A little further along the lane to Broadplat is Bix Manor (see p.114).

On the north side of the main road, and next to Bix church, is an unfenced area generally known as Bix Common. In fact, different portions of the area are owned by ten different individuals or families who are known as the Common Field Holders. They generally allow public access, and manage it as a single unit, usually for hay.

In Bix Bottom, a valley with a 'no through road' roughly parallel to the A 4130, there is the ruin of a Norman church, without a roof and partially covered in ivy. The Norman church was built to replace an earlier Saxon church, and served a hamlet that then existed in the valley. It was abandoned in 1875 and replaced by the church in Bix village itself, which was paid for by the Earl of Macclesfield. Further along the valley, about five miles from Henley, is the Warburg Nature Reserve which contains an abandoned rifle range used for practice by the Home Guard during the Second World War.

126 *The ruined Norman church at Bix Bottom, 2006.*

127 *Rebecca's Well, Crazies Hill, the village's main source of water until the 1940s. (Photograph, 2006)*

Crazies Hill

This village, whose name is thought to be derived from an old Celtic phrase for 'the hill of fresh clean water', has changed from extreme poverty to obvious affluence during the past 100 years, and largely during the past 50 years. For centuries, its only source of fresh water was a muddy spring on the hillside, and when this situation was appreciated by the Revd Greville Phillimore, in 1869, he raised funds so that a brick surround could be installed to improve the cleanliness of the supply. The site of the spring was previously known as Rebra's Well, which the Revd Phillimore concluded was an abbreviation of Rebecca's Well. He had a cross erected and introduced the new name, Rebecca's Well. Some years later, the local residents raised more funds for the well to be covered by a small open-fronted brick shelter designed by Gertrude Jekyll, the garden designer who lived nearby at Wargrave Manor around 1900. The shelter was subsequently decorated with a picture of the biblical Rebecca, probably paid for by Gertrude Jekyll herself. The well and its shelter still exist, having been renovated in the 1980s, and they are still only accessible along a woodland path, a path that is usually muddy.

In the early 1900s, nearly all the cottages in the village were occupied either by farm workers or by employees of one of the large houses nearby; and there were several shops, including a general store, a bakery and a sweet shop, in the village. Crazies Hill's change to affluence probably began in 1900 when Henley's old Town Hall was dismantled and re-erected there as a private house by Charles Clements, the Mayor of Henley, who then moved in with his family. The building was renovated in 2005-6 and is now known as Crazies Hall. When gas became available in Crazies Hill in 1912, and especially when piped water and electricity arrived in the late 1940s, the desirability of the village increased, resulting in the building of other large houses and the amalgamation of many of the existing cottages into larger properties.

During the Second World War, an area nearby at Cockpole Green became an airfield at which pilots were trained and test flights carried out, and buildings there were used for assembling Spitfire fighter planes.

Fawley

Fawley is a scattered village running along a Chiltern ridge, with the centre of the village more than two miles from Fawley Court, which is on level ground near the Thames. It is mentioned in Domesday Book as 'Falalie', and the church tower dates from the 1200s. The church itself was largely rebuilt in 1748 and many of the existing fittings and wooden panels were obtained at that time from a former mansion near Edgware that was owned by the Duke of Chandos. The wooden pulpit is reputed to have been carved by Grinling Gibbons. Many members of the Whitelock family, who owned Fawley Court during the 1600s, are buried in the church and churchyard, and there are marble effigies of Sir James and Lady Whitelock lying, under a canopy, in the south chapel. The families who succeeded the Whitelocks at Fawley Court, the Freemans until 1853 and the MacKenzies subsequently, both have large mausoleums in the churchyard. John Piper, the artist, is also buried there.

Following his purchase of a 300-acre estate at Fawley Hill in 1965, Sir William McAlpine set up a railway museum containing a collection of railway memorabilia, together with a mile-long working railway. As well as several signal boxes, there is a complete Victorian station, from Somersham in Cambridgeshire, that was dismantled and reconstructed at Fawley.

Hambleden

Excavations at Mill End, before 1914, uncovered the remains of a substantial Roman villa that had decorative tessellated floors and hypocaust heating (see p.5). Domesday Book records the existence of Hambleden manor, a fishery and a mill. The church was built in Norman times, though the font is thought to be Saxon. Inside the church is an alabaster monument, dated 1633, to Sir Cope and Lady D'Oyley and their children who lived at Greenlands, with four of the ten children holding skulls, an indication that they died before their parents. Over the centuries, the church has been subject to much rebuilding, the tower being added in 1719-21.

In the 1830s, the population of Hambleden parish was about 1,300 and many of the poorer people were involved in lace-making. At that time the village was reported to be a particularly healthy location, as several residents had been known to reach an age of at least 100. The village now consists mainly of brick and flint cottages, with the village pump and a chestnut tree on a triangular space in the centre. Most of the

128   *The memorial to Sir Cope D'Oyley and his family,*
dated 1633, in Hambleden church.

129   *Hambleden village in 1910.*

cottages in the village are included in the Hambleden estate that was bought by W.H. Smith in 1872 together with the house at Greenlands. The present Manor House, which is close to the church and dates from 1604, has been owned by the Smith family since 1923. W.H. Smith, his son and grandson, all lived either at Greenlands or the Manor House, and took an active interest in the life of the village. W.H. Smith provided land for a new cemetery for the village and was himself buried there in 1891. The cemetery also contains the grave of Major George Howson, who introduced the sale of artificial poppies to raise money for injured servicemen, and who died in 1936.

130   *The public ferry between Hambleden and Aston, that continued in operation until 1953.*

Until the mid-1930s, when piped water arrived, the residents of Hambleden depended on water from the central pump or from collected rainwater. Electricity became available at about the same time. There have been few recent changes in the village mainly because, in 1944, the 3rd Viscount Hambleden placed the estate under a National Trust covenant which restricts any building developments. One result of its relatively unchanged appearance has been that the village has often featured in film sets and television dramas. There was a threat to the ambience of the village in 2003 when the Hon. Henry Smith (son of the 4th Viscount) put the whole estate, except the manor house, up for sale. It was advertised in several lots for a total of £16.5 million. However, after much concern had been expressed, both locally and nationally, that the character of both village and estate would be irrevocably damaged, he decided to withdraw the sale. Nevertheless, the whole estate, excluding the manor house, was sold privately in 2007 for a sum reputed to be about £38 million.

At the end of the village nearest to the river is Hambleden Mill, which was used for the milling of flour until the 1950s and for many years, supplied flour by barge to the Huntley and Palmers biscuit factory in Reading. The mill has since been converted to apartments but, externally, is little changed. During the early 1900s, there was a ferry across the Thames both upstream and downstream of Hambleden lock. The former was an estate ferry that was large enough to carry a loaded cart with horses to and from land that was part of the Greenlands estate on the Berkshire side of the river. Downstream of the lock, at the end of a lane, there was a small ferry for pedestrians and horses, operated with a rope and later with a chain. This service enabled people to cross to the village of Aston with its inn, the *Flower Pot*, and continued in operation until 1953.

Harpsden

A hoard of coins dating from the first century BC, and found in Harpsden Woods in 1981, indicates human settlement before the Roman occupation. The remains of a Roman villa were discovered in Harpsden in 1941 near the 13th hole of Henley Golf Club. It is thought to have been built in about AD 280 and to have been abandoned, or much reduced in importance, about 100 years later. In medieval times, Harpsden

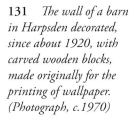

131 *The wall of a barn in Harpsden decorated, since about 1920, with carved wooden blocks, made originally for the printing of wallpaper. (Photograph, c.1970)*

was a manorial estate based on the site of the present Harpsden Court (see p. 122). The lord of the manor in 1204, John de Harpeden, was of sufficient importance and had sufficient resources to be required by King John to provide a knight and weapons towards the defence of Wallingford Castle. In Tudor times, the estate contained a number of tenanted farms, several of which were prosperous enough for the farmers to build brick houses. One of the earliest to be built was Hunts Farm, which has a cruck construction and is shown on a map of 1586.

The first church at Harpsden was built in the 1100s and for many years was regarded by the owners of Harpsden Court primarily as their private chapel. One of the rectors of Harpsden, John Webb, was responsible for building a spacious rectory about one mile west of the church in about 1617, and this was rebuilt and extended, in the early 1700s, to form the large red-brick mansion present today. The church itself had a major renovation in 1848. In 1857, the Hall family, who had sold Harpsden Court two years previously, paid for a village school to be built and this remained in use, latterly as an infant school, until 1996, when it was sold and converted to a house.

By the roadside, nearly opposite the entrance to Harpsden Court, there are two buildings, previously barns, with parts of their external walls decorated with a number of carved wooden blocks. The blocks were originally made for printing calico wallpaper and are thought to have been installed later in a panel in a shooting lodge on the Harpsden Court estate. Then, after the lodge had been demolished at the end of the First World War, Colonel Leonard Noble, who farmed at Harpsden Court, decided to use them to decorate the two barns. The floral patterns on the wood blocks are in the style of William Morris, though they may be earlier, perhaps Regency. They are still in relatively good condition, presumably as a result of being made from a tropical hardwood.

During the later 1800s, Bellehatch Park, a large house in the south-west of the parish, was the home of Archibald Brakspear of Henley Brewery, and he lived there till he died in 1909. Harpsden parish now includes Gillotts House, which forms part of Gillotts School, but until 1932 this was in the parish of Rotherfield Peppard. A Gillotts Farm is shown on a map of 1823, and in 1839, Gillotts House was owned by William Hodges. From the mid-1800s until 1919 it was owned by members of the MacKenzie family of Fawley Court. In 1880, Keith MacKenzie of Gillotts House owned an estate of between

2,000 and 3,000 acres. During the Second World War, while in the ownership of R.G. Bayldon, it was used as a Red Cross convalescent home for injured servicemen. Gillotts House was sold to Oxfordshire County Council in 1947, and in 1950 it became a Girls Technical School. Ten years later, this was amalgamated with Henley Secondary Modern School to become a co-educational comprehensive school (see p.99).

Henley Golf Course, also in Harpsden parish, was constructed between 1906 and 1908 on farmland that once belonged to the Harpsden Court and Bolney Court estates. Richard Blair, father of Eric Blair, better known as George Orwell, was the secretary of the golf club for a few years prior to 1917, when the family lived at Shiplake.

The present Village Hall in Harpsden was built with funds provided under the will of John Hodges of Harpsden Court, who died in 1924. John Hodges, who was a bachelor, also purchased and then donated land for the cricket ground, and founded the Harpsden Hall Trust which is still responsible for running the Village Hall. His father, who had acquired both Bolney Court and Harpsden Court, had become wealthy through his ownership of coal mines in Lancashire and John Hodges was a major benefactor to the village and its residents.

Lower and Middle Assendon

Lower and Middle Assendon are two of three hamlets in the Stonor valley, the third being Stonor itself. Stonor was known as Upper Assendon until the 1800s and is shown as such on the one-inch Ordnance Survey map published in the 1870s. However, the name derived from Stonor House was gradually adopted for the hamlet itself. Lower Assendon, which is close to the junction where the road to Watlington leaves the Henley-Oxford road, was for many years the most important of the three hamlets. It is reputed that during the stage-coach period its *Golden Ball* inn was patronised, and used as a hiding place, by the highwayman, Dick Turpin. In Victorian times, Lower Assendon had its own school, built and maintained with funds provided by Mr Newell Birch who lived at Henley Park.

Middle Assendon, which is now the largest of the three hamlets, began to expand in 1866 when a sawmill was established there, and in its heyday this employed nearly 100 men. The sawmill finally closed in 1966, and the modern houses in Mill Close were built on the site soon afterwards.

An unusual feature is the elusive Assendon stream which appears only occasionally but, when it does, it usually runs for several weeks or months before slowly drying out again. Its flow is induced by long periods of wet weather, sufficiently long and sufficiently wet to raise the water table in the Stonor Valley to above ground level. The stream generally rises as a spring in a field between Middle Assendon and Stonor, flows southwards along the valley to Lower Assendon and then in a ditch along the Fair Mile to Henley. From Northfield End it flows in an underground pipe to the Thames, joining the river between Phyllis Court and New Street. Sometimes the stream runs for only a part of the distance to Henley and disappears between Middle and Lower Assendon. Robert Plot, writing in 1676, noted that the stream ran only in occasional years but that, in 1674, 'several mills might have been driven with the current and, had not the town of Henley made some diversion, their Fair Mile must have been drowned for a considerable time'. Since 1960 it has appeared only once, during the winter of 2000-1, when it ran for several months and caused flooding in several houses and shops near Northfield End. It is thought to have appeared less frequently in recent decades than previously as a result of increasing amounts of water being abstracted from the surrounding chalk aquifer, and the consequent lowering of the water table.

Medmenham

Medmenham, which is mentioned in Domesday Book, was selected as the site of an abbey in 1145, and the abbey continued to be occupied until the Dissolution of the Monasteries in 1540. The buildings that replaced the abbey were bought in about 1750 by Sir Francis Dashwood of West Wycombe Park, and were used as a meeting place for the notorious Hell Fire Club, one of whose members was John Wilkes, a controversial journalist and politician. The Club held orgies and pseudo-religious rituals, but was eventually disbanded,

132   *The Assendon stream flowing along the Fair Mile, 1890s.*

reputedly after a practical joke by Wilkes. While Lord Oxford was addressing a prayer to Satan, Wilkes released a baboon dramatically disguised as the devil, and this had such an emotional impact on Lord Oxford that his mental state was seriously disturbed. Later, in the years around 1900, the buildings at Medmenham Abbey were converted to a hotel but they are now private houses. The present Medmenham church dates partly from the 1100s, while the tower was added in the 1300s.

By the riverbank is a monument erected in 1899 by Viscount Devonport to mark the occasion when he proved in court that the ferry at Medmenham was a public amenity.

The large house at Danesfield, now a hotel and country club, had an important role during the Second World War. It housed the Joint Intelligence Unit, where more than 2,000 people, mainly attached to either the RAF or the USAAF, were involved in assessing the information available from aerial photographs, many of which were obtained from flights made from RAF Benson.

Remenham

Remenham is now a small and rather scattered village, though the parish includes the settlements at Remenham Hill and Aston, and also the large country houses at Park Place and Culham Court. When Domesday Book was compiled, Remenham Manor was held directly by the King. It had a chapel under the jurisdiction of Hurley Priory and also a riverside mill. The church was built in the Norman period but has been much restored since then. During the medieval period, the manor formed part of Windsor Forest, and a hunting lodge was built where the house known as Remenham Court now stands. However, Remenham's significance declined after a major outbreak of the plague in 1625, when it lost much of its population. In 1768, Remenham Manor was purchased by Sambrook Freeman of Fawley Court.

Near the south door of the church is the tomb of Caleb Gould, who was the lock-keeper of Hambleden Lock for 45 years and who died in 1836 at the age of 92. He appears to have been an unusual character for his time. He was normally dressed in a long coat with silver buttons, and his tombstone is inscribed with the lines of John Gay (1685-1732): 'Life is a jest, and all things show it. I thought so once; but now I know it.' The lych gate of the church was erected by John Noble of Park Place in memory of his youngest daughter, Violet, who had died suddenly of scarlet fever.

A house in Aston was the home during the 1970s and '80s of Lord Hunt, who in 1953 led the first successful expedition to climb Mt Everest.

133   *The well cover, built to commemorate Queen Victoria's Diamond Jubilee, opposite the church at Rotherfield Greys.(Photograph, 2006)*

Rotherfield Greys

The village of Rotherfield Greys is well-known for its village green, with its attractions of spring-time cherry blossom and summer-time cricket. Greys Court, now a National Trust property, is about a mile away. The church contains an intact brass of a knight in full armour, commemorating Sir Robert de Grey, who died in 1387 and was the last member of his family to live at Greys Court. Sir Francis and Lady Knollys, who were the owners of Greys Court in the late 1500s, have the largest memorial in the church, the Knollys Chapel, which was built in 1605. The chapel contains their tomb made of coloured alabaster which suppports effigies of Sir Francis and his wife. On two sides are effigies of their seven sons and seven daughters, all in Elizabethan dress, and it was the second son, who became the Earl of Banbury, who arranged for the memorial and chapel to be built. Although Sir Francis is buried in the chapel, Lady Knollys, who was a cousin of Queen Elizabeth I, is actually buried at Westminster Abbey.

In 1823, the vicar, a Revd J. Ingram, attempted to raise money by cultivating poppies for opium in a small field near the church. Although the poppies were of good quality and the vicar was awarded a silver medal by the Society of Arts and Sciences for his method of collecting the opium, the yield was insufficient to provide a worthwhile profit.

The common land at Rotherfield Greys was enclosed in 1857. Opposite the church is a brick shelter that was erected in 1897 in commemoration of Queen Victoria's Diamond Jubilee. It was built as a cover for the village well, which had been provided by a member of the Stapleton family.

Henley Rural District Council built its first council housing at Rotherfield Greys in 1920. The land was donated by Sir Paul Makins and, in line with government recommendations, the houses were built to higher standards than those adopted by speculative builders of the time. For example, they had walls with cavity insulation, which was a relatively recent innovation. Nevertheless, the first occupants had to obtain their water either from the village well or from a large rainwater butt supplied with each house. The houses were also provided with substantial gardens of about 800 square yards, intended for growing vegetables.

134   Shiplake church and parsonage as illustrated in the Guide to Henley-on-Thames *of 1826.*

Shiplake

At the time of Domesday Book, the village of Shiplake did not exist and the area was part of the manor of Caversham that had been given to William Gifford as a reward for fighting with William the Conqueror at the Battle of Hastings. Even during the Middle Ages, there appears to have been no appreciable settlement at Shiplake, apart from that at Shiplake Court, though there was a ferry across the river to Wargrave. Later, a ferry near Bolney Court took people and horses across the river at a point where the towpath changed from the Oxfordshire to the Berkshire bank.

Shiplake developed within the manors of Bolney and Lashbrook, and grew substantially during the Victorian and Edwardian periods. The Bolney estate started to allow houseboats to be moored along the river bank, and later agreed to the owners of the houseboats having gardens next to their moorings. These arrangements encouraged wealthy families to spend their weekends and summer holidays on the river, often with their domestic staff so that they could continue to live in style and comfort and organise parties for their friends. The houseboats could be towed along the river when necessary, but they generally spent the winter tied up along the riverbank. In time, some of the owners of the houseboats were given permission to build houses on their gardens, and this trend was encouraged by the arrival of the railway in 1858. Around 1900, more land was sold for house building by the Bolney, Lashbrook and Crowsley estates, and Shiplake grew into a high-class residential area for commuters.

For the less wealthy, camping provided an alternative means of spending time by the river, and camping on an island by Shiplake Lock had become popular by 1888. The camp that still operates there from Easter till October was owned and operated by the Corporation of London until 1914 when it was transferred to the Thames Conservancy. The tents provided for the campers had wooden frames, wooden floors and heavy canvas coverings, and many of the people who used the camp, and those who still do so, are from families who have been visiting the island for several generations.

The parish church is where the poet Lord Alfred Tennyson was married in 1850. He was a friend of the vicar, and his bride was a cousin of the vicar's wife.

135   *The camp site on an island in the Thames at Shiplake.*

Wargrave

The name of Wargrave is thought to be derived from a combination of the terms for weir and grove, leading to the names of Weregreave and, by 1700, Wargrove. The manor of Wargrave is mentioned in Domesday Book as being owned by King William himself, and a village probably existed by that time. Later, the manor, which was almost certainly based at Wargrave Court, was held by the Bishop of Winchester. In the years around 1200, Wargrave rivalled Henley in importance, and in 1225 it was recorded as a borough with its own bailiffs and jurors as well as a market. Its importance declined after the building of Henley bridge, and the majority of Wargrave's population were employed in rural occupations until the Victorian era. A workhouse was built in the late 1700s.

Wargrave became well-known, and possibly rather notorious, during the years around 1790 as the home of Richard, the 7th Lord Barrymore. Richard's father died when he was only four and the Revd John Tickell and his wife then undertook, for payment, his upbringing and tuition. The Tickells lived at Wargrave Hall, and this remained as Richard's home base during the years he spent at Eton. Following a trend set by other members of his family, Richard Barrymore developed expensive tastes, and his liking for a flamboyant lifestyle was encouraged while he was at Eton by receiving an allowance of £1,000 from his maternal grandmother. In his mid-teens, with his brothers and a few friends, he indulged in practical jokes such as exchanging, at night, the signboards of various hostelries in the surrounding villages. When a little older, Richard Barrymore quickly became established as a 'man about town'. On leaving Eton, he decided to make Wargrave his home and bought a house at the bottom of Wargrave Hill. He then had built an impressive theatre that held about 700 people and was equipped with dressing rooms, expensive scenery and costumes, plus a beautifully furnished apartment for supper parties. It was considered to be the most splendid private theatre in England and probably in the world, and was attended by numerous members of the aristocracy,

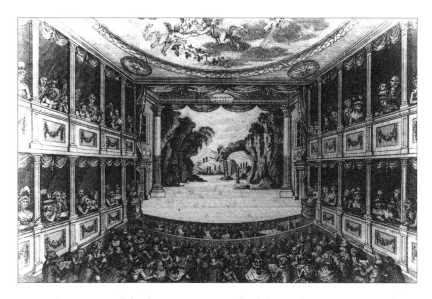

136   *Interior of the theatre at Wargrave built by Lord Barrymore, c.1790*
(from Robinson, 1894).

including the Prince of Wales. The total cost is reported to have been about £6,000 – 60 per cent of the cost of building Henley bridge, which was constructed at about the same time. Despite some reservations about the character of Lord Barrymore, Mrs Lybbe-Powys and her family, together with families from Fawley Court, Culham Court and Henley Park, attended a masked ball at the theatre and were highly impressed. Lord Barrymore was also an enthusiastic owner of horses, both for racing and hunting. However, his lifestyle resulted in bankruptcy, and this was followed by his being killed accidentally by his own gun in 1793 while he was escorting some French prisoners, and while he was still in his twenties. After his death, the sale of his possessions, which had already begun in order to pay off some of his debts, was completed. The theatre building was dismantled and the various component materials were all sold. A reminder of Lord Barrymore's time is the house 'Barrymore', built on the site of his own house near the *St George and the Dragon*.

In the Victorian and early Edwardian periods, Wargrave, like Shiplake, became fashionable, and many rather large family houses were built in and around the village. During the early 1900s, the residents of the village benefited from various gifts from a wealthy widow, Mrs Harriet Cooke Smith, gifts that included a parish hall (Woodclyffe Hall), six almshouses, a hostel and a recreation ground, as well as a village hall at Crazies Hill.

Wargrave attracted national attention again in 1914 when its parish church was largely destroyed by fire on the night of Whit Sunday, apparently owing to the action of a group of suffragettes. The fire appeared to have been started in several places by the wooden pews and, although the arsonists were not identified, there were suffragette slogans on three postcards left by the vestry window. A local resident, who went to the church while the fire was still burning, found the cards with handwritten comments such as: 'To the government hirelings and woman torturers … Defiance'. The fire was

137   *Wargrave church after an arson attack by suffragettes in June 1914.*

138   *Wargrave High Street, c.1900.*

first noticed at about 2.30 a.m. and, as Wargrave had only a manual fire pump, the fire brigades were called from Henley and Wokingham, but too late to save the building. However, the vicar arrived in time to rescue the parish records from the vestry before it was completely burnt. It may be surprising that the suffragettes should choose to attack a church, but they objected to the Church of England's support for the status quo, and unwillingness to change the bride's 'vow to obey' in the marriage service. It has been suggested that the attack on Wargrave church was a mistake, and that the suffragettes intended to target Shiplake church on the grounds that Lord Phillimore, who lived in Shiplake parish, was strongly opposed to women having the vote. When the First World War started, the suffragettes suspended their militant actions and, despite the war, the rebuilding of Wargrave church was completed in 1916.

Since the Edwardian period, Wargrave has continued to grow as a commuter village with easy access to Reading and Slough as well as to London.

Bibliography

Alasia, Valerie, 'The Henley Union Workhouse – 1834-61: national authority vs. local autonomy', *Oxfordshire Local History* 6 (1999)

Allen, Gemma, *The Story of The Henley College*, Tempus, Stroud (2004)

Andrew, Martin, *Henley-on-Thames, Town and City Memories*, The Francis Frith Collection, Salisbury (2005)

Anon., *Guide to Henley-on-Thames*, Hickman and Stapledon, Henley (1826)

Anon., *Guide to Henley-upon-Thames,* Hickman and Kinch (1838)

Armstrong, Walter, *The Thames from its Rise to the Nore*, Vol.1, Virtue & Co., London (c.1884)

Bailey, J.F., *A Phoenix Once Again*, Higgs & Co., Henley (1974)

Bailey, John, 'A Millennium of Sport', *Henley Standard* Special Millennium Supplement, 7 January 2000

Baldwin, Jan, *Henley Heritage*, Gresham Books, Henley (1994)

Boardman, Carl, *Foul Deeds and Suspicious Deaths around Oxfordshire*, Wharncliffe Books, Barnsley (2004)

Bolland, R.R., *Victorians on the Thames*, 3rd edn, Parapress Ltd, Tunbridge Wells (1994)

Brett, Lionel, *Landscape in Distress*, The Architectural Press, London (1965)

Brooks, John, *Henley on Thames: A view from the Bridge*, Jarrold Publishing / W.H.Brakspear and Sons plc, Henley (2000)

Burden, V., *Chiltern Villages*, Spurbooks Ltd, Bourne End (1972)

Burn, John Southerden, *A History of Henley-on-Thames in the County of Oxfordshire*, Longman & Co., London (1861)

Burnell, R., *Henley Royal Regatta – A Celebration of 150 Years*, William Heinemann, London (1989)

Climenson, Emily J., *A Guide to Henley-on-Thames* (1896) republished by Gresham Press, Henley

Climenson, E.J., *Passages from the Diaries of Mrs Philip Lybbe-Powys of Hardwick House, Oxon, AD 1756 to 1808*, Longman Green & Co., London (1899)

Cooper, John, *An Account of the Charities under the Management of the Corporation of Henley-upon-Thames*, Thomas Day, London (1858)

Cottingham, Ann, *The Hostelries of Henley*, Ann Cottingham, Shiplake (2000)

Cottingham, Ann H.G., *The Town of Henley, its Town Halls and its Town Councils*, Henley Archaeological and Historical Group, Henley (2000)

Cottingham, Ann and Fisher, Hilary, *Henley on Thames – A Pictorial History*, Phillimore & Co., Chichester (1990)

Delaney, P. (ed.), *The Second Book of Wargrave*, Wargrave Local History Society (1998)

Dils, Joan A., 'Henley and the river trade in the pre-industrial period', *Oxfordshire Local History* 2 (1987)

Eccles, J. R., *Historical Notes on the Parish of Bix & Assendon* (1997)

Ellis, Sian, *Around Henley-on-Thames in Old Photographs*, Alan Sutton, Stroud (1992)

Ford, Reginald W., *A Description of Binfield Heath and the Surrounding District*, R.W. Ford, Reading (c.1960)

George, Kester, *The Millennium History of Harpsden*, Harpsden Hall Trust (2000)

Graham, Malcolm, *Oxfordshire at War*, Alan Sutton, Stroud (1994)

Gray, Charles, *Born on Chiltern Slopes: Reminiscences of Hambleden*, Pheasants Hill Press, Hambleden (2003)

Gray, R. and Griffiths, S. (eds), *The Book of Wargrave*, Wargrave Local History Society (1986)

Hepple, Leslie W. and Doggett, Alison, *The Chilterns*, Phillimore & Co., Chichester (1992)

Hewitt, L., 'A Study of Gillott's House and Wood', thesis submitted to Berkshire College of Education, Reading (1972)

Hollingworth, G., *The Story of Henley*, Local Heritage Books, Newbury (1983)

Jessup, Mary, *A History of Oxfordshire*, Phillimore & Co., Chichester (1975)

Karau, Paul, *The Henley-on-Thames Branch*, Wild Swan Publications, Upper Bucklebury (1982)

Kemplay, John, *The Thames Locks*, Ronald Crowhurst, Chipping Campden (2000)

Kendal, R., Bowen, J. and Wortley, L., *Henley in the Age of Enlightenment*, River & Rowing Museum, Henley (2002)

Kendal, R.J. and Cottingham, A.H.G., 'Investigation of the Stable at the King's Arms Public House, Market Place, Henley-on-Thames', *Oxfordshire Local History* 4 (1996)

Kinch, E., *Guide to Henley on Thames and its Vicinity*, E. Kinch, Henley (1866)

Law, Brian R., *Eye and Dunsden: Two Centuries of Change*, Brian Law, Shiplake (2001)

Leslie, George D., *Our River*, Bradbury, Agnew & Co., London (1888)

Macleod, Michael, *Land of the Rother Beast: A South Oxfordshire Chronicle*, Skye Publications/ Ridgeway Press, Pangbourne (2000)

Malpas, F.J., 'Roman Roads South and East of Dorchester-on-Thames', *Oxoniensia* (1987)

Mayo, The Earl of, Adshead, S.D. and Abercrombie, P., *Regional Planning Report for Oxfordshire*, Oxford University Press (1931)

Mitchell, V. and Smith, K., *Branch Lines to Henley, Windsor and Marlow*, Middleton Press, Midhurst (2002)

Moloney, Colm, 'Excavations and Building Survey at Bell Street, Henley-on-Thames, 1993-1994', *Oxoniensia* 62 (1997)

Oxford Health Authority, *Public Health in Oxfordshire: the Past*, Oxford Health Authority (1998)

Pearman, M.T., *A History of the Manor of Bensington*, Elliot Stock, London (1896)

Perkins, Angela, *The Phyllis Court Story*, Phyllis Court Members Club, Henley (1983)

Peters, George H., *This Glorious Henley*, Independent Press Ltd., London (1950)

Philips, Robert, *Henley and its Volunteer Forces*, Cressrelles Publishing Co. Ltd, Peppard Common (1980)

Pilling, J. and Woods, L., *Henley-on-Thames, Past and Present*, Sutton Publishing, Stroud (2000)

Pitt, David, *Henley's Hospital*, David Pitt, Henley (2004)

Plot, Robert, *The Natural History of Oxfordshire*, Oxford (1676)

Port, Bill, *The Well-Trod Stage of the Kenton Theatre, Henley-on-Thames*, Robinswood Press, Stourbridge (2005)

Railton, Margaret, *Early Medical Services in Berkshire and South Oxfordshire from 1740*, Polmood Publications, Reading (1994)

Ransom, Elizabeth (ed.), *Life in Our Villages, Past and Present: Binfield Heath, Crowsley, Shiplake Cross, Lower Shiplake*, Henley Publishing, Henley (2001)

Read, Brian, *Henley Rural – A History of Henley Rural District Council, 1894-1932*, ELSP, Bradford-on-Avon (2003)

Rivers-Moore, C.N., 'Further excavations in the Roman house at Harpsden Wood, Henley-on-Thames', *Oxoniensia* 16, 23-7 (1951)

Roberts, Cecil, *Gone Rambling*, Hodder and Stoughton, London (1935)

Robinson, J.R., *The Last Earls of Barrymore*, Sampson Low, Marston & Co., London (1894)

Rodwell, K. (ed.), *Historic Towns in Oxfordshire*, Oxford Archaeological Unit, Oxford (1974)

Salter's Guide to the Thames, Alden & Co. Ltd, Oxford (1936)

Sheppard, Francis, *Henley-on-Thames in old Picture Postcards*, European Library, Zaltbommel, Netherlands (1983)

Sherwood, J. and Pevsner, N., *The Buildings of England: Oxfordshire*, Penguin Books, London (1974)

Shinn, Judy, *Ashurst Morris Crisp: a Radical Firm*, Granta Editions, Cambridge (1997)

South Oxfordshire District Council, *District Plan for Henley-on-Thames* (1979)

South Oxfordshire District Council, *Henley Conservation Area Character Study* (2004)

Tomalin, G.H.J., *The Book of Henley-on-Thames*, Barracuda Books, Chesham (1975)

Turner, J.B.W., *Henley: The Best Organised Picnic in Europe*, Management Update Ltd., Shrewsbury (1989)

Tyack, Geoffrey, 'The Rebuilding of Henley-on-Thames, 1780-1914', *Oxfordshire Local History* 3 (1989)

Umfreville, J.H., 'The Comings and Goings of Charles Clements', *South Oxfordshire Local History* 5 (1998)

Williams, A. and Martin, G.H. (eds), *Domesday Book: a Complete Translation*, Penguin Books, London (2002)

Wilson, D.G., *The Thames: Record of a Working Waterway*, Batsford, London (1987)

Woodward, F., *Oxfordshire Parks*, Oxfordshire Museum Services, Woodstock (1982)

Index

Page numbers that refer to illustrations only are in **bold**

Ordnance Survey map of Henley published in 1927